WH
AND OTHER  MARINE MAMMALS

by
GEORGE S. FICHTER

Illustrated by
BARBARA J. HOOPES AMBLER

GOLDEN PRESS • NEW YORK
Western Publishing Company, Inc.
Racine, Wisconsin

595

FOREWORD

Interest in marine mammals in past centuries concerned mainly their commercial value. Many were harvested so heavily for meat, hides, fur, oil, and other products that they are now listed among the world's endangered species. Steller's Sea Cow was slaughtered into extinction by 1768.

In recent years it has been discovered that these mammals rank among the most intelligent of all animals. The largest are gentle giants; many have effective means of communicating with each other, and many are remarkably responsive to training. As a group, they are indeed among the most interesting of all creatures on land or in the sea. They have captured the attention and affection of people everywhere, even those who have never seen or will never see them in their natural habitat.

This book is a brief survey of the major groups and species of marine mammals. Only a fragment of this fascinating subject can be touched upon in a limited space, but these pages point the way to learning more.

Special thanks are due Barbara J. Hoopes Ambler for her magnificent art, Dr. Vincent B. Scheffer for reading the manuscript and making certain it was on course, and Caroline Greenberg, Remo Cosentino, and Henry Flesh for their expert engineering from start to finish.

G.S.F.

CONTENTS

MARINE MAMMALS 4

WHALES, DOLPHINS, AND PORPOISES 6
How cetaceans developed. The way cetaceans breathe. How cetaceans give birth. The senses of cetaceans. The way cetaceans sleep. How cetaceans swim. Migratory journeys of cetaceans. The whaling industry. The need for conservation. The training of marine mammals in captivity. Looking out for the interests of cetaceans.

BALEEN WHALES 34
Right Whales 36
Rorquals, or Fin Whales 40
Gray Whales 52

TOOTHED WHALES 54
Beaked Whales 62
Sperm Whales 66
Narwhal and White Whale 70
Porpoises 76
Dolphins 96
River Dolphins 100

MANATEES AND DUGONG 100
Manatees 102
Dugong 104
Steller's Sea Cow 106

SEA LIONS, WALRUSES, AND SEALS 108
Eared Seals 111
Walruses 124
Earless Seals 128

CARNIVORES 144
Otters, Weasels, and Their Kin 144
Bears 148

WHALE WATCHING 152

ANIMAL WELFARE ORGANIZATIONS 154

MARINE MAMMAL EXHIBITS 156

MORE INFORMATION 157

SCIENTIFIC NAMES 158

INDEX 159

MARINE MAMMALS

About 120 of the more than 4,000 species of mammals live in the sea. These are the cetaceans (whales, dolphins, and porpoises), the pinnipeds (sea lions, walruses, and seals), the sirenians (manatees and Dugong), and two carnivores (the Sea Otter and the Polar Bear). The principal species in each group, shown in the family tree of mammals, are described and illustrated in this book. All marine mammals, even those so fishlike in appearance that they were once believed to be fish, share features that make them members of the class Mammalia.

All mammals are warm-blooded—that is, their body temperature is regulated internally and is independent of the environment. The young are carried internally by the female and nourished through an umbilical cord until their birth. They are then suckled (fed on milk) from their mother's mammary glands. Marine mammals also possess hair, which is as unique to mammals as feathers are to birds. Some marine mammals, such as the Sea Otter, Polar Bear, and several pinnipeds, have thick fur. Others, such as the

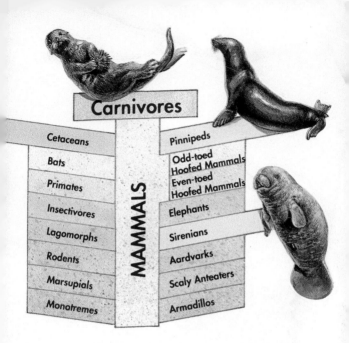

Carnivores

MAMMALS	
Cetaceans	Pinnipeds
Bats	Odd-toed Hoofed Mammals
Primates	Even-toed Hoofed Mammals
Insectivores	Elephants
Lagomorphs	Sirenians
Rodents	Aardvarks
Marsupials	Scaly Anteaters
Monotremes	Armadillos

cetaceans and sirenians, are covered with hair during an early stage of development but have a thick hide and only a scattering of bristles as adults.

Like their land-dwelling relatives, marine mammals have lungs and must breathe air. Whales, some of which are capable of diving more than a mile deep and can remain submerged for an hour or longer, must nevertheless surface to replenish their oxygen. Their blood is circulated by an efficient four-chambered heart. (Fish, in comparison, get their oxygen directly from the water by means of gills, and their less-efficient heart has only two chambers.) The brain of marine mammals is large and well-developed in contrast to the brain of lower classes of mammals.

5

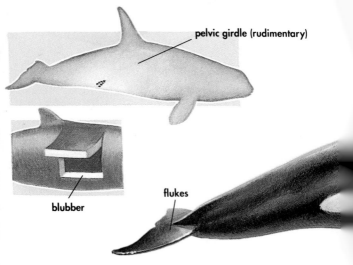

pelvic girdle (rudimentary)

blubber

flukes

WHALES, DOLPHINS, AND PORPOISES

Order Cetacea

All of the cetaceans, which total approximately 75 species, are exclusively aquatic, more completely so than are any other mammals. At no stage of life do they leave the water. Cetaceans range in size from the gigantic Blue Whale, the largest creature that has ever existed, to medium-sized dolphins and porpoises, some of which are only slightly more than 3 feet long. Typically a cetacean's head is joined to its body without a distinct neck. Except in a few species, the head cannot be turned independently. Characteristic of mammals, however, cetaceans do possess seven neck vertebrae, though much compressed. In some of the larger whales these are fused into a single disc only a few inches thick.

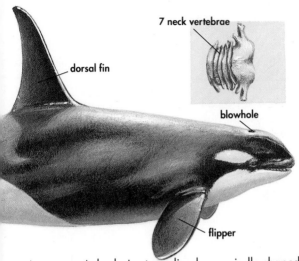

7 neck vertebrae

dorsal fin

blowhole

flipper

A cetacean's body is streamlined, or spindle-shaped, and in some species the head may be extended into a "beak." Many kinds have a definite dorsal fin consisting of a thick folded ridge of skin without a bony support. This feature adds to their general fishlike appearance. A cetacean's front legs are flippers, with no exposed claws or digits. A much reduced bony structure for a pelvic girdle is still in evidence internally, but external hind limbs are lacking. The tail, which provides the principal driving force for swimming, is extended into a broad horizontal appendage, separated into two flukes by a notch in the middle. The thin skin lacks hairs except for a few bristles around the mouth and on the belly in some species. Underneath the skin is a thick layer of blubber (mostly fat) that serves as a heat insulator as well as a food reserve. Blubber may be 2 feet thick in some of the larger whales and may account for more than 40 percent of the animal's total weight.

CETACEANS DEVELOPED from mammals that lived on land, their return to the sea commencing perhaps 60 million years ago. Fossil evidence is scarce, and so the precise and complete picture of cetacean evolution remains a bit of a mystery.

The sea has notable advantages over a land habitat. For one thing, food is more plentiful and easily obtainable. The sea is also a more uniform environment, lacking the large and sudden shifts in temperature that commonly occur on land.

An early sea-dwelling cetacean named *Basilosaurus* still had features marking it as closely related to the land dwellers. Some 60 feet long, it had an exceptionally long tail that made it so snakelike it was first classified as a reptile. Its hind legs had already disappeared, but its short, flipperlike front legs terminated in five digits. The nostril, or blowhole, was not yet centrally located on the top of the head. This unusual sea-dwelling mammal, now extinct,

may or may not have been a direct ancestor of modern-day cetaceans.

Fossils show that the extinct forms of cetaceans had teeth differentiated into molars, canines, and incisors, like most mammals today. Modern cetaceans, some of which have a fossil history almost as long as the group to which *Basilosaurus* belonged, are divided into two suborders: the baleen, or whalebone, whales (Mysticeti) and the toothed whales (Odontoceti).

Toothed whales have simple teeth—conical, peglike, and all similar. Some species have several hundred teeth, others as few as two. Whales do not use their teeth for chewing but as effective tools for holding prey until it can be maneuvered into position for swallowing.

In baleen whales, teeth are lacking. Instead, these species have baleen, or whalebone, forming a screen that sieves tiny animals out of water taken into the mouth. These animals provide nourishment for the whales.

skeleton of *Basilosaurus*

9

A CETACEAN BREATHES AIR through nostrils located on the very top of its head—one opening (or blowhole) in toothed whales, two blowholes in the baleen whales. The blowhole is closed by valves when the cetacean goes beneath the surface. Since there is no open connection between the nasal passages and the mouth as there is in other mammals, whales, dolphins, and porpoises can take water into their mouth with no danger of having it get into their lungs.

The instant a whale or other cetacean reaches the surface, the blowhole is exposed to the air and opened. The animal immediately exhales, or "blows." The heated air, under pressure and filled with water vapor, blasts into the cooler air of the atmosphere where it condenses into the characteristic "spout." In large whales, the spout may rise to more than 20 feet.

"Thar she blows!" was the jubilant cry of whalers on the lookout for their quarry. Experienced whalers could identify

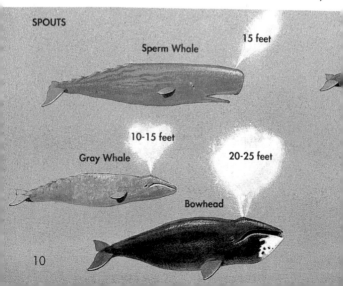

SPOUTS

Sperm Whale — 15 feet

Gray Whale — 10-15 feet

Bowhead — 20-25 feet

the kind of whale and its size by the shape and height of the spout. Whale watchers today can identify not only species but individuals by their spouts.

Some cetaceans can hold their breath for longer than an hour. Their very large lungs are stretched throughout the full length of their capacious abdominal cavity and are divided into as many as three times more air-holding sacs (alveoli) than are the lungs of land-dwelling mammals. Of equal importance is the fact that a cetacean can empty its immense lungs more completely than can land-dwelling mammals and then replenish them quickly with a fresh supply of air. In addition, the hemoglobin (red pigment) in a cetacean's blood has a greater capacity for holding oxygen than does the hemoglobin of land-dwelling mammals. All of the openings to the respiratory system—including the blowholes and the bronchial tubes—can be tightly shut by muscles.

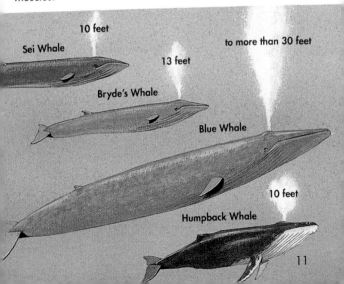

10 feet

Sei Whale

13 feet

to more than 30 feet

Bryde's Whale

Blue Whale

10 feet

Humpback Whale

CETACEANS GIVE BIRTH at sea. Typically only one calf is born; occasionally but rarely there are twins. In the larger species, there is a lapse of two years after the birth of the calf before the cow can bear again. In most cases, the calf is born tail first. As soon as the umbilical cord breaks, the young calf must get to the surface for its first breath of air. It can swim immediately, but often the mother gives it a boost in the right direction on this first and highly important trip. She will support the calf at the surface until it is fully adjusted to its sudden independence from the womb. Until this moment it has been warmed by the mother's amniotic fluid, but now it is in the cold sea.

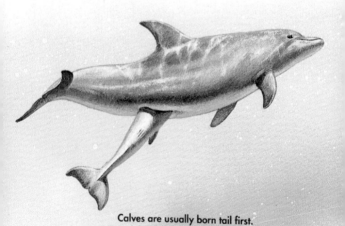

Calves are usually born tail first.

Calves suckle under the water while the mother swims.

Nursing

Baleen whale mothers nurse their calves for about six months to a year. Toothed whales nurse for a year and a half to two years. A calf suckles under the water as the mother swims along slowly. Each mammary gland, one located on the right and one on the left just ahead of the tail, is hidden in a pocket of skin. The nipples are extruded by muscles during nursing.

Milk is produced in the glands and held in reservoirs. When the calf begins to suckle, the mother forces the milk out quickly. This shortens the time required for suckling so that the young can get back to the surface to breath. A cetacean's milk is very rich—about ten times higher in calories than cow's milk. The calf gets ample energy to sustain its rapid early growth. A baby Blue Whale, for example, may double its weight in as short a time as a week. (Human babies, by comparison, double their weight in roughly four months.)

13

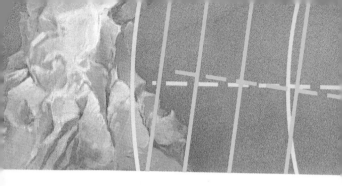

SENSES OF CETACEANS developed to meet the demands of the aquatic habitat. In proportion to their body size, for example, cetaceans' eyes are small, protected from the salt water by a waxy secretion. Their vision is good but is not a highly important sense. Cetaceans have totally lost the sense of smell.

Although a cetacean lacks external ears, its hearing is acute. It can detect sounds for hundreds of miles in the sea. All cetaceans emit sounds for communication and some for navigation as well. The sounds are produced in the nasal passageways, not by the larynx. The "melon" of the Sperm Whale (p. 54) focuses or beams the sounds just as a lens focuses light.

Communication

The sounds vary with the species, but in general they are produced at two frequency levels. Sounds made at low frequency may be heard by people as squeaks, grunts, clicks, or whistles. These noises are used when the animals are "talking" to each other. The chatter is continuous when the animals are swimming in a group. The frequency of these sounds is typically no higher than 15,000 cycles per second, but they may be even lower than 1,000 cycles,

Cetaceans identify objects underwater by echolocation.

both well within the range of human hearing. The haunting mating songs of the male Humpback Whale are at this frequency, and interestingly, the males vary their songs from year to year. Sometimes a male will sing for 20 hours or longer, with brief stops only for breathing. Are they singing what females most like to hear?

Echolocation

Another type of sound begins at a frequency of about 20,000 cycles per second, but this is mostly beyond the range of human hearing, which ends at about 25,000 cycles. Some sounds have been recorded at frequencies higher than 200,000 cycles per second. These high-frequency sounds, given off in short pulses, "echo" back to the animal from any objects in their surroundings. The echoes tell the cetacean where to find food and also guide it toward or away from objects. This echolocation system, similar to that used by bats and sonar-equipped ships, is remarkably accurate. A cetacean can determine not only the size and distance of objects but also their shape and structure. It is believed that migrating Bowhead Whales are guided around ice obstructions by scout whales traveling miles ahead of the herd.

MOST CETACEANS SLEEP occasionally while floating close to the surface. This is called "logging." As long as the top of the head is above the surface, they can continue to breathe while sleeping with no danger of drowning. Some of the larger whales sleep so soundly that ships run into them or they drift into shallows. Dolphins and porpoises seem to take frequent rests and naps but apparently never go into deep sleep.

SWIMMING in cetaceans is accomplished by up-and-down movements of the broad horizontal flukes, the body moving little from side to side. This is in contrast to fish, in which the tail moves from side to side and, for the majority (particularly the fast swimmers), the body supplies most of the power for swimming. Fish utilize their side fins for steering. Cetaceans steer by shifting the plane at which their flukes move through the water, though the paddlelike flippers assist in steering and also in balancing.

Most of the large whales cruise at 4 to 5 miles per hour. For short distances they may accelerate to 20 miles per hour, a few going even faster, but they do not maintain this speed for long. Many of the dolphins and porpoises, however, swim at 20 or even 30 miles per hour for short periods of time.

Swimming power is from up-and-down movement of broad flukes.

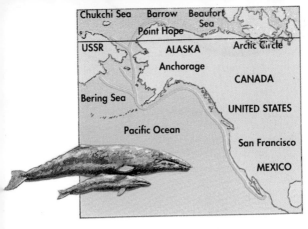

Migration route of the Gray Whale

MIGRATION Many cetaceans make long migratory journeys between feeding and breeding areas. Best known of the migrants are the giant whales that were the quest of whalers. These hunters had to know where to look for whales in each season. They knew that the big whales spent their winters in warm or temperate waters, then returned to cooler waters in summer. These trips took the whales thousands of miles in a year.

The giant baleen whales find their food at least 20 times more plentiful in the cooler waters than in warmer seas. A big Blue Whale, for example, can stuff its stomach with as much as 4 to 8 tons of krill (small shrimplike crustaceans) per day, in this way building a reserve of energy, stored as blubber, for its months of fasting on the breeding grounds. Most of the whales take their trips in groups (pods or gams) made up of families, and they travel to and from the same general areas of the sea year after year.

WHALES WERE KILLED for subsistence by Eskimos and other shore-dwellers in early times. The people ate whale meat and blubber, used the oil as fuel for cooking and lighting, and made implements and decorative objects from the teeth and bones. Centuries ago whaling became an important maritime industry, but modern whaling methods ultimately exceeded the capacity of whales to replenish themselves. A number of whale species are now near

New England whalers hunting off the coast of Hawaii are shown in this 19th-century print.

extinction. In effect, the whaling industry put itself out of business by becoming too efficient and too greedy.

Some chroniclers say the first European whalers were the Norwegians, but most credit the Spaniards with making whaling a business. Soon the Dutch and the English became commercial whalers, too. Whaling was also important for centuries in Japan.

Soon after the settling of North America, whaling fleets

from the Americas began to invade the seas. In the mid-1800s, the United States' whaling fleet consisted of about 750 vessels, more than twice as many as the vessels of all other countries combined.

Nantucket, New Bedford, Gloucester, Marblehead, Provincetown, New London, Southampton, and many other towns on the east coast of the United States were built primarily around the whaling industry. Fortunes were made by some of the whale hunters and by those who merchandised whale products. Whalers took whatever whale was within striking distance of their harpoons, but the most sought after were Bowhead, Right, Humpback, Sperm, and Blue whales.

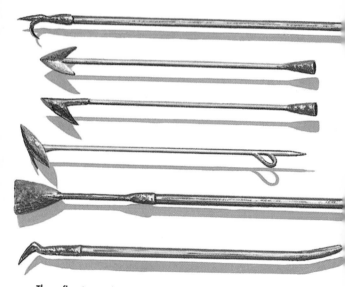

These flensing tools and harpoons were used by early whalers.

Firing harpoons from guns and cannons began about 1868.

Whaling was a most dangerous and adventuresome enterprise. In the early days, whales were hunted from shore stations. Whalers sighted the animals that came close to the coast and then set out in small boats to chase them for the kill. When the hunters were close enough, they threw the heavy, sharp harpoon by hand, then attached ropes to killed or exhausted animals and towed them back to shore for processing.

Whales were also hunted in the open sea with larger vessels. Struck whales sometimes managed to capsize boats, hitting them with their broad, powerful flukes in their struggles to get free. Later, harpoons were fired from cannons, and their tips were fitted with explosives.

Whales were doomed when whalers took to the open sea in huge factory ships and fleets of fast, smaller boats

21

that did the job of killing and towing the catch. Airplanes and helicopters were also employed to locate the whales and guide the whalers to their quarry. No whale was too large to be killed or processed. No whale was safe anywhere. No thought was given to conservation. The industry was ruled by greed.

Whole whales could be taken aboard on slipways at the stern of factory ships. They were immediately butchered with modern, mechanized equipment, and the products were refrigerated or rendered for oil. The ship then continued on its slaughter route. With whales nearing extermina-

Modern whaling ships not only destroyed the whales, but also the industry.

tion in the Northern Hemisphere, the factory ships concentrated in Antarctic waters where the job of destruction was eventually nearly completed. In one season during the 1950s, factory ships processed more than 40,000 whales—compared to an annual production of fewer than 50 per season during the 1850s, before the days of factory ships.

The whaling industry has now become history—or nearly so. If any harvests are to be allowed in the future, they must be rigidly controlled by strictly enforced international agreements.

A kill of Sperm Whales brought alongside a whaling ship to be processed.

CONSERVATION and its importance to the saving of cetaceans came into focus gradually. In large measure this was due to poor knowledge of total populations and to the slow rate at which cetaceans reproduce.

When whalers no longer found hunting for a particular species profitable, they turned to another. They thought that they were simply having "bad years," as farmers sometimes have poor crops due to unfavorable weather. In fact, the whalers had hunted a species to such a low population level that its very survival was endangered. But there were no statistics to tell them this.

When methods of censusing whales improved and population dynamics was better understood, the real plight of cetaceans was finally known. Authorities began sounding alarms. Getting an effective remedy was particularly difficult, for cetaceans live in international waters. Controls require international agreement and cooperation.

In 1946, the International Whaling Commission was established. In the beginning it had one representative from each of more than a dozen nations. By 1988 there were more than 40 members. The IWC's purpose is to establish rules and regulations to safeguard whale populations, utilizing the advice provided by experts. Often the interests of the whalers has been a greater concern than the survival of the whales. More troubling has been the inability of the IWC to get its proposals accepted against the wishes of a nation. Huge factory ships, mainly from Russia and Japan, continued to hunt for those few whales still remaining.

Slowly an understanding has come that protection of whales is necessary to prevent total destruction of their populations. The regulations suggested by the Commission are reluctantly being accepted. Perhaps enough time is left to prevent extinction of some of the most magnificent creatures ever to have inhabited the earth.

A stranded 1,200-lb. baby Sperm Whale is lifted onto a flatbed truck to be transported to the Dolphin Research Center.

Whaling, however, is not the only problem faced by cetaceans. They suffer, for example, when the waters where they feed become polluted and their food is destroyed. Porpoises and dolphins come into regular conflict with commercial fishermen, who say that these animals eat too many fish and damage their fishing gear. There are times, too, when mysterious maladies strike in epidemic proportions. In the summer of 1987, for example, dolphins along the east coast of the United States died in large numbers as the result of a strange infection.

Fortunately, more and more people are aware of whales, dolphins, and porpoises and are willing to invest time and money to save them from extinction. Both government and private agencies are involved in these efforts.

TAMED AND TRAINED dolphins and their kin have delighted people for many years. To their credit, these gentle animals have seemed to try to establish a friendly relationship with humans.

Ancient coins and vases show a boy riding a dolphin, but this depiction was generally believed to be mythical. Yet persistent stories from around the world told of these friendly sea mammals appearing among people at beaches and frolicking with them. The animals sometimes allowed the most courageous humans, particularly youths, to hold onto their dorsal fin in order to get a ride. In return, the animals liked to have their bellies scratched or their backs stroked.

Other tales told of porpoises charging into a school of prowling sharks and sending the fearsome fish on their way, thus sparing the life of a swimmer or a wading fisherman. A front-page story once told of a woman caught in

Jumping through hoops is a standard stunt for performing dolphins.

Dolphins swim at a high speed, then jump in unison.

an undertow that was carrying her out to sea. Suddenly she was nuzzled by something and, within seconds, was rolled onto the beach, beyond the power of the tugging waves.

Did the dolphin save the woman by intent or by accident, simply pushing at her playfully and out of curiosity? No one really knows, of course, but authorities doubt that the dolphin, though intelligent, could actually recognize the woman's plight. Some, however, insist that the dolphin knew precisely what it was doing.

Dolphins

Dolphins first performed in marine exhibits in the 1930s, when they were brought to Marineland of Florida at St. Augustine. Since then, dozens of similar shows in the United States and throughout the world have used them to star in outdoor extravaganzas. "Flipper," the Bottlenosed Dolphin in a motion-picture and television series of the 1960s, further popularized his species. People who had never seen dolphins in their natural habitat began to appreciate their gentleness, cleverness, and seeming high intelligence.

Once the most feared creatures in the sea, Killer Whales are now star performers at sea-life exhibits.

Killer Whales

Now another popular performer at marine exhibits, the Killer Whale was for many years ranked as the most ferocious, voracious, and dangerous beast in the sea. Hunting in packs like wolves, Killer Whales are indeed fearsome. Sharks, dolphins, seals, whales—no animal in the sea can be safe from their attacks. Swimmers were continually warned about them. As late as the 1970s, in fact, survival booklets for military personnel listed the Killer Whale as the most dangerous creature that could be encountered at sea—in spite of the fact that no Killer Whale had ever been known to harm a human. Indeed, a sort of comradeship with these big beasts had been developing for nearly a decade.

In 1964, a sculptor commissioned to make a life-sized replica of a Killer Whale for a museum set out to get a real model. He wounded a Killer Whale, then towed it back to port. When it responded to his attention and did not display ferociousness, despite having been treated badly, the sculptor became very attached to it. Many visitors came to see the hapless captive, and though it did not live long, it performed an invaluable service as a missionary for its kind. Now people began to understand that the Killer Whale was not only approachable but also amazingly manageable. Soon the Killer Whale moved into the limelight at many marine exhibits. A confident trainer might even put his or her head into the creature's gaping mouth, demonstrating the animal's docility. At Sea World in Orlando, Florida, a Killer Whale produced an offspring for its owners, and the baby was soon performing with all the adeptness of its mother. It has never known the vast world of the open sea.

Conflict with Commercial Fishermen

Until dolphins endeared themselves to people with their showmanship, their general image was negative, due in large measure to commercial fishermen who referred to them as "herring hogs" and accused them of stealing more than their share of fish. They claimed that these animals ate their own weight in fish every day. If this were true, those in captivity would work on starvation diets, for they manage all of their explosive enthusiasm and exuberance on 20 pounds or less of fish each day. Such performers disprove earlier misconceptions and captivate the public in the process. Few other animals have built such widespread popularity for themselves in so short a time.

When conservationists pointed out that tuna fishermen were deliberately drowning about 300,000 dolphins every year in their nets, public wrath brought the entire tuna fleet to a temporary halt. The nation was righteously indignant. Sadly, dolphins were paying with their lives after leading the fishermen to bountiful catches. Tuna and dolphins are typically found together, although this relationship is not well understood. Neither feeds on the other, but it is evident that both somehow benefit from the association—until nets draw tight around them!

Performers

What can performing dolphins do? Almost everything but talk, and some believe that dolphins may even be taught to speak. One group has suggested that these creatures could eventually be taught a human language. Unquestionably, they do faintly mimic the human voice. In marine exhibits they commonly make sounds like those they hear around them. But in these shows they display other, more fascinating talents.

Dolphins will respond to both visual and spoken commands. They work for rewards—a fish for every well-performed act. But to the animals, work seems almost to be play. They appear to enjoy themselves from start to finish in every show, and they are perfectionists. When they make a mistake, they rarely need to be reprimanded or told by the trainer to repeat a trick. They know from experience that they get no fish until an act is well done, and so they voluntarily give it another try.

On command from its trainer, a dolphin will balance a ball on its nose and then throw the ball to a companion who catches the ball on *its* nose and throws it back. The first dolphin may then flip the ball onto its head and let it roll down its back to its tail, this time using its broad flukes to throw the ball. When finished with their act, the dolphins may swim to the trainer, each extending a flipper for a "handshake" before picking up their fish.

Their leaps are always spectacular, a dolphin weighing 300 to 400 pounds easily pushing itself 15 or more feet into the air to hurdle a crosspiece or grab an object from the top of a pole. Nowadays, too, visitors are awed at the sight of gargantuan Killer Whales erupting from the water. With unbelievable deftness, one of them will hurtle through the air and pluck an object from the trainer's mouth.

Dolphins are also creative, sometimes inventing their own games to play with spectators. They may select one person who for some reason looks cooperative and then toss him or her an object from the pool. If the person throws it back, a game is underway. The object goes back and forth, always to the same person and always thrown with astonishing accuracy.

Performing dolphins speed across the water by "tail walking."

Little Bit, a former "Flipper" star, gives a boy a ride.

Dolphins seem to like almost anyone, though certain colors seem to disturb them. If someone dressed in black is standing at the pool rail, a dolphin may drench that person with a wave or swim close enough to squirt the person with a mouthful of water. When performing such a prank, the dolphins are obviously pleased. They "chuckle," make clacking noises, and applaud themselves by clapping their flippers.

Left alone, dolphins play games to amuse themselves, rewarded only by their own pleasure. Given a feather, a dolphin may carry it to a jet of water coming into the tank and release it into the stream. As the feather shoots off, the dolphin gives chase and retrieves it. Sometimes a second dolphin will join in the fun, one carrying the feather to the jet and letting it loose, the other catching it. Whether leaping through hoops onstage or playing on their own—at whatever they do, dolphins wear an infectious "smile" that delights all who watch their antics.

What dolphins do in these shows is the result of intensive schooling by their trainers. The most effective trainers are those who have a natural "way with animals"—that understanding between trainer and beasts that seems almost inborn. With intelligent, responsive dolphins, training is considerably easier than with many other animals. To keep the performer in trim, their "school" has sessions seven days a week. When performing, the experienced, dependable veterans get the limelight. Trainees or apprentices do lesser stunts and wait their turn for top billing.

Keeping Watch

Some people voice concern about dolphin performers being deprived of their freedom and held prisoners in cramped tanks. These dedicated people monitor the animals and their living conditions. Fortunately, in today's major exhibits, the animals have enough room to feel comfortable. They are well fed, and their medical needs are met immediately. Most importantly, the exhibits focus attention on the special adaptations and needs of cetaceans for their aquatic life.

Some people concerned for the welfare of dolphins and other sea mammals have been especially critical of those who train them for military duties. The animals are not, however, trained as killers, nor are they trained to be killed as carriers of grenades and bombs. Dolphins were first used by the U.S. Navy as offshore sentries during the Vietnam War. They were also employed in the Persian Gulf to locate mines and to detect movements of saboteurs at work underwater. Military trained dolphins demand payment only in fish and also in the affection they get from their appreciative handlers.

BALEEN WHALES

Suborder Mysticeti

Whales of this suborder do not have functional teeth. Instead, they have baleen, or "whalebone," a flexible horny substance—white in some whales, black, yellowish, or two-toned in others. In a large whale, more than 300 plates of baleen hang down like stiff curtains from the upper jaw on each side of the mouth. A plate may be as much as 12 feet long, and a foot or more in width. The outer edge is straight, fitting tightly against the jaws when the mouth is closed. The inner edge (or tongue side) is extended into bristles that form a hairlike fringe of thin tubes. Baleen continues to grow throughout the whale's life, replacing material worn away by the action of water and the tongue.

When feeding, a whale swims into a swarm of small crustaceans with its mouth open. As the whale closes its mouth, water is forced out at the sides and through the sievelike screen of baleen. Small crustaceans or even small fish become caught on the bristly fringes. The whale then uses its tongue to move them into its throat for swallowing. Even the largest whale has a throat passageway not much larger than an orange. It is not large enough, at any rate, to accommodate anything the size of the Bible's Jonah.

The tough, pliable baleen was one of the highly valued commercial products obtained from whales. It was used in corsets and in similar products in which stiffness with flexibility was important. It has been replaced by plastics.

Baleen whales can be distinguished from the toothed whales by their having two blowholes instead of one. When they blow, the twin spouts are distinctive. Baleen whales are gentle giants of the whale clan.

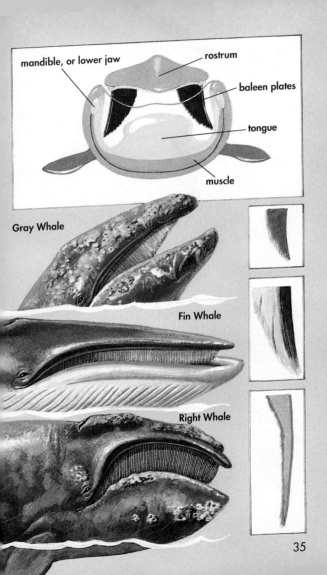

mandible, or lower jaw

rostrum

baleen plates

tongue

muscle

Gray Whale

Fin Whale

Right Whale

35

RIGHT WHALES

Family Balaenidae

These were called "right" by early whalers because they were the best—the "right"—ones to hunt for their rich yield of oil and whalebone. In addition, they did not struggle as violently as other species, and conveniently, they floated when dead. Right whales have a large head, and there are no grooves in the throat or on their abdomen. A distinctive feature is the lack of a dorsal fin (except in the Pygmy Right Whale). The baleen of the right whale is exceptionally long. In the Bowhead, for example, each plate may measure as much as 12 feet.

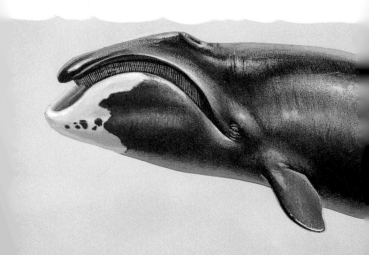

BOWHEAD WHALE measures about 50 (occasionally 60 or more) feet long, its giant head accounting for a third of its total length. This big whale, which may weigh as much as 100 tons, is almost totally black, the color grading to a gray around the tail and flippers. It has white under its chin and sometimes on its highly arched upper jaw. The baleen is dark gray to black.

Once abundant in arctic waters, the Bowhead Whale is now rare. It is found in arctic seas, occasionally ranging as far south as the Gulf of St. Lawrence and the Bering Sea. The slow-swimming Bowhead Whale travels in groups of a few animals but may occasionally band together in large herds. The Bowhead once went by the name of Greenland Right Whale.

RIGHT WHALE, once the most common whale of temperate seas, has been reduced in numbers to only a few thousand animals. It is about the same size as the Bowhead Whale but with a smaller head and thus less baleen. The function of its "bonnet," a horny growth on its arched upper jaw, is not known. The bonnet is typically infested with parasites, and barnacles grow on it.

A closely related species was once equally abundant from Alaska to southern California. It, too, is now endangered. Another right whale inhabits the cool seas of the Southern Hemisphere.

PYGMY RIGHT WHALE, to 20 feet long but usually less, lives off the coasts of South America, Australia, and New Zealand. It has never been common, and little is known about its habits. Unlike other right whales, it has a dorsal fin. Each of its more than 200 baleen plates is only about 2 feet long.

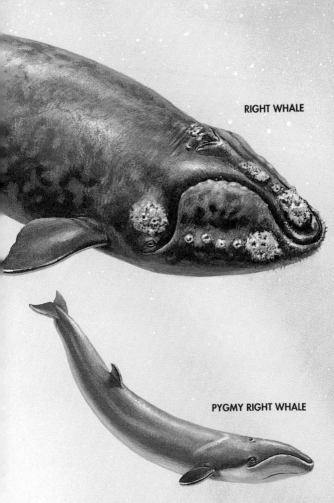

RIGHT WHALE

PYGMY RIGHT WHALE

RORQUALS, OR FIN WHALES

Family Balaenopteridae

These whales have a triangular dorsal fin set well back near the tail and a series of folds or pleats under the throat. The head is short and flat as compared to the large, high-arched head of right whales. The smaller mouth contains less baleen, which is shorter and stiffer than the baleen of right whales. Fast swimmers, these whales were dangerous quarry for whale hunters.

FIN WHALE may be 80 feet long but is usually shorter, and may weigh as much as 60 tons. "Fin" refers to its curved, 2-foot dorsal fin.

Razorback is another name for this whale because of the sharp ridge down its back.

The Fin Whale's most unusual feature is its asymmetrical coloring. The right side of the lower jaw is white, the left side dark. The tongue is darker on the right side than on the left, and the baleen is also bicolored, the plates on the left bluish gray and those on the right light yellow.

Fins can swim as rapidly as 30 miles per hour, and harpooned animals often towed whaleboats. In winter, these whales migrate to warm temperate seas, where they mate and the females give birth. In summer, they return to polar waters where their food (mostly small crustaceans but also small fish) is plentiful. They may consume 2 tons or more of food every day. As a result of whaling harvests, the Fin Whale is now an endangered species.

BLUE WHALE, the largest animal that has ever lived on land or in the sea, may measure more than 100 feet long and weigh as much as 200 tons. Females are slightly larger than the males. A Blue Whale's gigantic head is about a quarter of the animals's total length.

Because of its streamlined body, the Blue Whale appears to be a fast swimmer. Ordinarily its top speed is only about 15 miles per hour, and it can continue swimming at this speed for two hours or longer. Harpooned whales, however, have been known to go twice as fast, though they cannot maintain this faster speed for a long time. This great whale is also a deep diver. Typically it travels less than 350 feet under the surface, but it may dive to

well over 1,000 feet deep. When it blows on resurfacing, the columnlike spout may rise to more than 30 feet.

A wary and nearly solitary creature, an adult Blue Whale is easily frightened. Whale hunters learned to approach as silently as possible to prevent their quarry from being scared away. Under the surface, a Blue Whale may make moaning sounds that are detectable for 50 miles or farther.

Young Blue Whales are not as cautious as are the

43

adults. Inquisitively they will swim close to boats. During the whaling days, this curiosity was often a fatal mistake.

The Blue Whale is slate-blue above and lighter below. Often the underside is yellowish due to growths of diatoms on the whale's pleated or grooved undersurface. Another name for the Blue Whale in days gone by, in fact, was Sulphur-bottomed Whale, and coincidentally, the abundant diatoms are the principal food of the krill that sustain the big whales.

There are 100 or more pleats or grooves on the whale's underside. When these are stretched, they give the whale's mouth much greater capacity for taking in the large quantities of water from which it strains its food. The pleats also increase the size of the whale's chest in respiration, making it possible to take in an enormous quantity of air for its long stays underwater.

This giant animal subsists on a diet of krill, which are shrimplike crustaceans seldom measuring more than 2 inches long. In the summer months, Antarctic waters teem with krill. Hundreds of square miles of the ocean are turned reddish brown by swarming clouds of the crustaceans. The sea becomes a nutritious "soup" that the Blue Whale can

Krill, none more than 2.5 inches long, feed the largest animal now alive or that has ever existed.

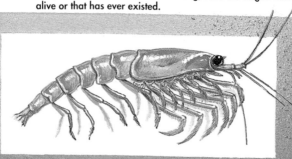

partake of simply by opening its mouth. A big whale's stomach may contain more than a ton of krill, and in a day's time, the whale may consume 4 tons or more.

During the winter months, the whales move to northern waters that are warmer. During these months, the whales do not eat. They survive by living off their ample blubber, having accumulated as much as 20 tons during their months of feeding. During the winter months, too, the Blue Whales mate.

Females, or cows, bear a single calf, usually every two years. The calf may be more than 20 feet long at birth, and it grows rapidly, generally adding a ton of weight every week or so. Within a year it has doubled its length, and within five years it is sexually mature and ready to bear young of its own.

Only a few thousand Blue Whales still exist, whaling having reduced their numbers from an estimated 250,000. They are now protected by international agreements, but all countries do not abide by the regulations. Unfortunately, too, the regulations are not always based on the best biological data, and represent the interests of whalers as much as, or more than, the welfare of the whales.

SEI WHALE may reach a length of 60 feet and weigh as much as 30 tons. It has a strongly arched upper jaw, like the Bowhead Whale. The large dorsal fin is recurved on its hind margin, and the pleats or grooves on its underside do not go aft of the short flippers. The Sei Whale is gray to black on its upper surface and white below, but the white does not extend to the tail. The baleen is black, its fringes white and so fine they are woolly or hairlike—extremely effective in trapping the small crustaceans on which the

whale makes most of its meals. It also traps and eats small fish.

Found in all seas, the Sei Whale moves toward the equator in winter and toward cooler water in summer. It is less common in polar waters than the Fin, Humpback, or Blue whales. The Sei Whale is believed to be the fastest swimmer of all the fin whales, possibly achieving speeds exceeding 20 miles per hour, and this speed gave it protection from whalers for many years.

MINKE WHALE, the smallest of the fin whales, measures about 25 feet long. Its yellowish white-fringed baleen is less than a foot long. The Minke Whale is blue-gray above and white below, with a distinctive white patch on the outer side of each flipper. The dorsal fin is high and curved, the snout pointed. This whale frequently travels in small schools that swim into bays and estuaries or close to coasts. When these whales jump, they generally fall back on their side, making a large noise and splash. The Minke Whale is found in both the Atlantic and Pacific, ranging from warm equatorial to icy polar waters.

BRYDE'S WHALE

BRYDE'S WHALE, about 40 feet long, lives in warm to temperate seas throughout the world. Its most distinctive feature is its baleen, which is white streaked with gray and black. Because its fringes are so brittle that they cannot serve effectively as a sieve, this whale feeds mainly on small schooling fish. Bryde's Whale is slimmer and more streamlined than any of the other fin whales. Three ridges extend from the snout back to the area of the blowholes. This medium-sized whale commonly bears scars from attacks by sharks. Brydes's Whale was never abundant and did not contribute significantly to the whaling industry.

HUMPBACK WHALE, to 50 feet long, has an exceptionally large head, accounting for nearly a third of the animal's total length. Numerous wartlike tubercles on its head have

bristles or hairs in their center, and there are as many as 25 throat grooves, or pleats. The small dorsal fin is located slightly aft of the midpoint between the head and tail. The exceptionally long flippers—to 12 feet or more—are scalloped on their front margins. The Humpback Whale is black above and whitish below, including the flippers and flukes. Its baleen is gray-black. Found in all seas, only a few thousand Humpback Whales are believed to survive today, the animals having been hunted to near extinction.

This whale sometimes leaps completely out of the water in an act called breaching. Its 50 tons crashing back onto the surface can be heard for miles. In reentering the water,

its body is bent—or "humpbacked." It also beats the surface with its flukes, which is called lobtailing. Some of these antics are believed to be related to courtship. When males sing (p. 15), they characteristically hang head down in the water.

GRAY WHALES

Family Eschrichtiidae

GRAY WHALE, the only species in its family, grows to a length of 45 feet and may weigh more than 30 tons. It has only two to four pleats, or grooves, under its throat, and its yellowish baleen is more than a foot and a half long. The head is narrow and the dorsal fin so indistinct that it can scarcely be distinguished from the bumps, or "knuckles," on its back. As its name indicates, the basic color is gray, but there are many lighter marks over the body.

The Gray Whale was once common throughout the

North Pacific, ranging as far south as Japan and California. It was hunted to near extinction, but the protection provided by the International Whaling Commission since 1947 appears to have helped it make a comeback to its original population of 15,000 to 20,000. Gray Whales often cruise close to shore and play in the surf, sometimes in groups of 100 or more individuals. In autumn the whale leaves its feeding grounds in the Bering Sea, traveling southward to the southern coast of Mexico where it breeds. The cows then give birth and defend their calves so aggressively that the Gray Whale was called "Devilfish" by early whalers. In spring the whale makes its return journey, the round trip for some individuals totaling 14,000 miles (p. 17).

TOOTHED WHALES

Suborder Odontoceti

All of the many species in this suborder have teeth in either the upper or the lower jaw or in both. In most, the teeth are simple and conical, useful for catching and holding prey but not for chewing. Some dolphins have 300 or more teeth, more than any other mammal. Other members of this suborder are nearly toothless or have only a few specialized teeth. In several species the head bulges, even extending beyond the end of the jaws. Filled with an oily, fibrous tissue, this so-called "melon" is apparently part of the sound-detecting and focusing system. Toothed whales have a single blowhole.

Nearly all of the toothed whales travel in groups, or pods, some of which consist of hundreds of individuals. Sounds, some above the range of human hearing, are utilized to keep in contact with other members of the herd. All of the toothed whales are carnivorous, making their meals mainly of squid and fish. Most toothed whales are small, averaging about 6 feet in length, but the Killer Whale may reach a length of 30 feet. The Sperm Whale may attain a length of 60 feet, making it the largest of the toothed whales.

BEAKED WHALES

Family Ziphiidae

Members of this family have a distinct snout, and most of them have a high, domed forehead. Under the throat are two (sometimes more) deep grooves that nearly meet under the chin but separate as they pass toward the rear of the body. The hind edge of the triangular dorsal fin is concave, and the flippers are slender. Unlike other cetaceans, the wide flukes are not deeply notched in the center.

Most of the beaked whales live in the open sea, where they travel in pods. They are known for their habit of swimming and diving in unison. Normally they remain submerged for 15 to 30 minutes then surface to blow, but harpooned animals have been known to stay underwater for an hour and a half or longer.

GOOSEBEAK WHALE, to 25 feet long and weighing as much as 4 tons, travels in schools which have been seen in all oceans. The animals swim in unison at the surface with their backs exposed, diving and then surfacing together to blow. They commonly remain submerged for half an hour or longer. Their principal food is squid. The Goosebeak does not have as high a forehead as the Bottlenosed Whale (p. 56), and it appears more streamlined. It varies from dark brownish or bluish above to light below.

BOTTLENOSED WHALE, about 25 feet long and weighing as much as 4 tons (though usually less), travels in schools generally consisting of approximately a dozen animals. This whale's principal food is cuttlefish.

The Bottlenosed Whale's forehead bulges prominently, becoming increasingly exaggerated as the animal grows older. Inside this hollow bony dome, or "melon," is a reservoir of spermaceti (p. 62), which made this whale the most commercially valued of the beaked whales. The young are born gray or even blackish. As they grow older, they become a much lighter color, first splotched with yellowish white and then finally covered by yellowish white over the entire body.

The Bottlenosed Whale winters in the mid-Atlantic and spends its summers in the cool waters of the Arctic. The closely related Southern Bottlenosed Whale lives in the Southern Hemisphere. Whalers considered the Bottlenosed Whale one of the most dangerous, for when harpooned, the whale would dive immediately, often to a depth of 2,000 feet or more. Unless the line attached to the harpoon was extremely long and remained free-running until the animal had reached the end of its dive, the plunging whale could take a whaler's boat under. The whale itself could remain submerged for an hour and a half or longer. After a deep dive, a whale stays at the surface for as long as 15 minutes, blowing and regaining its breath.

BAIRD'S WHALE

BAIRD'S WHALE, to 40 feet long and weighing as much as 10 tons, is the largest of the beaked whales. It lives in the North Pacific, from as far south as Japan and California northward to the Bering Sea. Two of the teeth in its lower jaw are extraordinarily large, and its "melon" is pronounced. Baird's Whale is gray or brownish black, sometimes with white blotches on the belly.

A closely related and somewhat smaller species inhabits the cold seas of the Southern Hemisphere, particularly off New Zealand.

DENSE-BEAKED WHALE

DENSE-BEAKED WHALE, to 14 feet long, roams temperate and tropical seas throughout the world but is abundant nowhere. At each corner of its mouth is an arched bulge (most prominent in males) in which a huge tooth is rooted. The tooth may be as much as 8 inches high and 3 inches wide. In males these teeth typically protrude from the jaw, but in females they remain covered by the gum. The Dense-beaked Whale is grayish black above, with scattered blotches of a lighter color, and it is uniformly lighter on the belly.

SOWERBY'S BEAKED WHALE, about 15 feet long, is the most common of more than half a dozen rare species in its genus. Some of these whales, none of which is more than 20 feet long, are known only by a few individuals. As they are mainly dwellers of the open ocean, they are not normally seen. Sowerby's Beaked Whale lives in the North Atlantic. It was given the name "Cowfish" when an individual that was stranded off Le Havre, France, bellowed like a cow. Sowerby's Beaked Whale has a long snout and a rather slim, streamlined body. It has no outstanding color

STRAPTOOTHED WHALE

or markings, but there is a noticeable bulge in its head just in front of the blowhole.

All of its close relatives (True's Beaked Whale, Pacific Beaked Whale, Straptoothed Whale, and others) have a long snout and deep grooves under the throat. In the Straptoothed Whale, the pair of flat teeth grow longer as the animal becomes older. In time these teeth may curve over the upper jaw and prevent the animal from opening its jaws fully. Because they live in deep, cold waters, little is known about the habits of these whales.

61

SPERM WHALES

Family Physeteridae

SPERM WHALE is probably the most familiar of all whales because of the male's high, square-fronted head. In a large male, which may be 60 feet long, the head accounts for more than a third of the animal's length. Cows are only about half as large as the males. The male's enormous head consists mainly of a reservoir containing spermaceti, a white oily mass believed to act as a sort of cushion against the great pressure at the depths to which the whale dives. The Sperm Whale is known to dive more than a mile deep. When it dives, the whale lifts its flukes high into the air, then "sounds," or dives, almost straight down into the water. It may remain submerged for an hour or longer before surfacing to "blow." Only Beaked Whales (p. 54)

dive deeper or stay under the surface for a longer period of time.

The single "S"-shaped blowhole, on the left side near the front of the head, directs the spout forward at an angle. The lower jaw does not extend as far forward as the front of the head, which adds to the beast's unusual appearance. The Sperm Whale has no dorsal fin, only a series of bumps—the first and most prominent located about two thirds of the way from the snout to the tail. Compared to the whale's size, its flippers are extremely small.

This giant, which consumes more than a ton of food every day, feeds on squid and cuttlefish that it hunts in deep water. Its battles with the Giant Squid are well marked by the scars on the whale's body where the squid's hooked suction cups have dug in deeply. Scars inside the whale's stomach suggest that a squid continues to fight even after being swallowed.

A Sperm Whale's usual color is black, or nearly so, but the female may be gray. The occasional albino offspring inspired Herman Melville's novel *Moby Dick*. At birth a Sperm Whale is nearly 15 feet long. The mother rolls onto her side near the surface so that the baby can breathe as it nurses.

A large Sperm Whale could yield as much as 4,000 gallons of oil. The spermaceti, which becomes a white, waxy solid in air, was used in ointments. Sperm oil, also taken from the head, made an excellent lubricant for precision machinery. The meat was eaten, and the teeth, which may be as much as 7 inches long and weigh half a pound, were carved into ornaments. The most unusual product from the Sperm Whale is ambergris, found floating free in the ocean or washed onto the shore. It can also be taken directly from a whale's intestines, where it apparently forms due to an irritation. Fresh ambergris is a blackish, foul-odored mass. When dry, it is lighter in color and has a musky odor. It was once used in producing the most expensive perfumes, for the gumlike ambergris would easily absorb and retain delicate odors. In 1912, a half-ton mass of ambergris removed from a Sperm Whale sold for nearly $112,000.

These huge whales communicate with a wide range of clicks, squeaks, groans, and other sounds. If attacked or frightened they give off cries that travel for miles and serve as a warning to other whales.

Sperm Whales are essentially whales of tropic and temperate seas. They travel in pods that nowadays are comprised of only a few animals, but in times past consisted of hundreds of individuals. Of the great whales, however, it is now the most abundant, the world population believed to exceed half a million. This is nevertheless only about a third of its original population.

PYGMY SPERM WHALE, to 12 feet long and weighing only about 1,000 pounds, does not have a large head. It is shaped more like a porpoise. The short lower jaw and a pale mark resembling a gill cover on each side of the head give it a sharklike appearance. Like its large cousin, however, it does have a spermaceti case, though a much smaller one. The Pygmy Sperm Whale has a dorsal fin. This whale, which has always been rare, occurs in warm and temperate seas throughout the world. It often becomes stranded on shore.

The Dwarf Sperm Whale is smaller than the Pygmy Sperm Whale, measuring only about 6 feet long. It also has a proportionately higher dorsal fin. Like the Pygmy Sperm Whale, it occurs in warm and temperate seas throughout the world. As a species, it has been recognized only since the 1960s.

NARWHAL AND WHITE WHALE

Family Monodontidae

NARWHAL, to 16 feet long, is grayish white—literally corpse colored. *Nar*, its Scandinavian name, means corpse. Commonly the animals are spotted with black.

The Narwhal has no dorsal fin. Its most distinctive feature is the male's tusk. (A female rarely has one.) This tusk usually develops only on the left side, but occasionally a

When it surfaces to breathe, the White Whale emits a low trill, so melodious at times that the Eskimos call it the Sea Canary. Like the Narwhal, the White Whale lives only in the cold waters of the Arctic, but it may also travel up northern rivers like the St. Lawrence. Schools of these whales often contain hundreds of animals.

PORPOISES

Family Phocoenidae

Porpoises, sometimes confused with dolphins (p. 76), are distinguished by their lack of a beak, their flat teeth, shorter, blunter flippers, and stockier body. Both porpoises and dolphins are small toothed whales, most measuring less than 15 feet long. Porpoises inhabit cool, coastal waters and may travel far up rivers. Their name is derived from the French for "sea hog," as they were once considered a delicacy—literally a fish that could be eaten on days when the church forbade eating meat. Porpoise was a favorite food of the royalty.

Porpoises feed on fish, and not uncommonly they get caught and drown in the nets of commercial fishermen.

HARBOR PORPOISE usually measures less than 6 feet long and weighs about 100 pounds, occasionally more. The triangular dorsal fin sometimes has warty tubercles along its

front edge. The teeth are uniquely spade-shaped. The Harbor Porpoise is bluish black above, including the blunt, oval flippers, and white below, usually grayish toward the middle of the belly. Generally it travels in schools of half a dozen or so animals. An occasional school may contain as many as 100. Except with its own kind, the Harbor Porpoise is not particularly sociable. It lives in the North Atlantic and North Pacific, staying in the shallow water close to shore. Here they have to contend with fishermen's nets, boats, and pollution. It does bring Harbor Porpoises close to people, however, who see them playing and surfacing regularly to breathe. Relatives of the Harbor Porpoise are found off the coast of South America.

71

DALL'S PORPOISE is strikingly marked—black with a white belly and flanks. It measures up to 7 feet long and has a stout body with small flukes and flippers and a low dorsal fin. Dall's Porpoise lives in the North Pacific where it travels in schools ranging in size from a dozen or fewer to several hundred. It is a swift swimmer, regularly following

ships. It jumps only seldomly but sends a spray of water into the air when it surfaces.

True's Porpoise, inhabiting the western North Pacific, is similar to Dall's. The white saddle-shaped marks on its belly are larger than those on Dall's Porpoise, and there are also differences in the teeth and skeleton.

FINLESS PORPOISE is distinguished by its lack of a dorsal fin. In the ridge replacing the fin is a row of tubercles. The Finless Porpoise lives off the coasts of India and China. It seems to prefer murky waters and often ascends rivers for hundreds of miles. Most individuals are uniformly gray, but some are black.

The Finless Porpoise measures about 5 feet long. Its flippers are large and pointed, and the flukes are distinctly notched. It is ordinarily a slow swimmer and moves along a course with rapid changes in direction. It rarely jumps, nor does it remain submerged for much longer than a few minutes before surfacing.

DOLPHINS

Family Delphinidae

More than 60 species comprise this largest family of cetaceans. They range from the open sea to coastal areas and into rivers. Most dolphins feed just below the surface. They are excellent swimmers, and some will leap clear of the water. Compared to porpoises (p. 70), dolphins have a more streamlined body, and most have a distinctly beaked snout and many sharp, conical teeth. They generally travel in schools and may aid each other in fighting off intruders. They have been known to kill large sharks by ramming them repeatedly. Some authorities also believe they use bursts of sound to stun fish or other prey.

SADDLEBACK DOLPHIN, to 8 feet long, is found in warm and temperate seas throughout the world. It is abundant, usually traveling in schools, and like many of its relatives, enjoys riding the bow wave of a ship. At intervals it frolics in the water nearby, then returns to the ship to let the bow wave do the work of pushing it along. In sudden dashes, the Saddleback may attain a speed of 30 miles per hour, and it cruises comfortably at about half this rate.

This graceful animal, its 6-inch beak clearly separated from its forehead by a groove, is dark bluish black or brown above and white below. A ring of black encircles each eye, and wavy bands of white, gray, and yellow mark the sides. The high, tapered dorsal fin is recurved on its hind margin. The Saddleback feeds on fish it catches in the vicelike interlocking of its more than 100 teeth.

Like porpoises and dolphins generally, the Saddleback has long had a reputation for saving drowning people. Friendly but wary, the animal often sports playfully around

swimmers and divers. Occasionally, whether intentionally
or accidently, it has been known to roll drowning people
into the surf and ashore, or it has managed to help them
stay afloat until they rallied sufficiently to help themselves
or until rescuers reached them. Survivors have testified that
dolphins did indeed provide this sort of aid. Dolphins are
also known to aid their own comrades, keeping them afloat
when they are in danger of drowning. The Saddleback
Dolphin is the animal made famous in the Greek tale of the
boy who rode a dolphin to school every morning and then
home again each afternoon.

77

BOTTLENOSED DOLPHIN, to 12 feet long, is the most commonly seen of the dolphins. It is abundant in the Atlantic, but it may appear in warm temperate seas anywhere in the world, generally staying near the coasts. Schools of Bottlenosed Dolphins often consist of hundreds of individuals. Easily captured and then tamed, this gentle dolphin is the one seen in most marine exhibits. It is taught to jump, throw balls, and put on other performances that demonstrate its agility and intelligence. Studies are underway to

learn the "language" of its whistles, squeaks, chirps, and grunts. Some scientists are convinced that if we are ever able to communicate with other animals it will be with the dolphins first. A Bottlenose Dolphin was the star of the film and television series *Flipper*.

The Bottlenosed Dolphin is grayish black above and white below, including its lower jaw. The beak, or "nose," is short, and the dorsal fin curves backward, ending in a rather sharp point.

SPOTTED DOLPHIN

SPOTTED DOLPHIN, to about 9 feet long, is mainly seen off the east coast of North America but is not common. It is metallic blue above and has a gray belly. Its spots (and stripes in some) are distinct only at close range.

The closely related Slender Dolphin lives in warmer Atlantic waters to the south. The wide-ranging Spinner Dolphin of warm seas is so named because it "spins," or twists its body, when it leaps from the water. The Spinner Dolphin's upper jaw is black, its body gray, and its belly white. The dorsal fin and the flukes are dark. About half a dozen other members of the same genus live in the Caribbean, Indo-Pacific, and other warm waters. All have long, narrow beaks and small, pointed teeth.

COMMERSON'S DOLPHIN, 4 to 5 feet long, also goes by such common names as Piebald Porpoise, Le Jacobite, and Skunk Dolphin. The last name comes from its color pattern—head and tail black, entire midsection of body white, a striking coloration. Commerson's Dolphin and several closely related but less common species are found in waters of the Southern Hemisphere. All have small beaks and triangular, round-tipped dorsal fins.

COMMERSON'S DOLPHIN

NORTHERN RIGHT-WHALE DOLPHIN

NORTHERN RIGHT-WHALE DOLPHIN, to 9 feet long, has a short, slim beak and no dorsal fin. It lives in the North Pacific. A similar and closely related species, the Southern Right-Whale Dolphin, lives in the Southern Hemisphere, particularly in Antarctic waters. The southern species is dark above and white below, the northern species similar but with the contrasts less sharp. Both are streamlined, swift swimmers that prefer the open sea. Often they leap out of the water. The northern species travels in large schools.

81

PYGMY KILLER WHALE, to 8 feet long, inhabits warm waters of the Atlantic, Pacific, and Indian oceans. It is rare, most of those reported having been caught off Japan. Totally dark grayish black except for its white lips and a patch of white near its anus, the Pygmy Killer Whale has a rounded head, no beak, and few but large teeth. The dorsal fin is high, the flippers long and slim. The original identification of this species was made from skulls in the 1800s. It was not until the 1950s that a whole animal was seen.

IRRAWADDY DOLPHIN, to 8 feet long, has a high, rounded forehead and no beak. Its small dorsal fin is sharply recurved, and the long flippers are straight-edged and almost triangular. Nearly uniformly slate blue, the Irrawaddy Dolphin has no distinct markings.

As its name implies, this dolphin is common in the Irrawaddy River region of Burma. It also occurs off Thailand and commonly appears elsewhere along the coast of Southeast Asia. Often it travels hundreds of miles up rivers.

WHITE-SIDED DOLPHIN, to 9 feet long, lives in the North Atlantic where schools consisting of as many as 1,000 animals are sometimes reported. It uses the numerous small teeth in its short, dark beak to catch and hold fish, squid, and other foods. The tail is keeled or ridged above and below, the flukes notched, and the flippers sickle-shaped. As its name indicates, this dolphin can be distinguished by its white sides. A yellowish streak above the white extends from the middle of the body to the tail. Like its relatives and many other cetaceans, the White-sided Dolphin commonly "lobtails," or pounds the surface with its tail. It is very active and often jumps.

The White-beaked Dolphin, closely related, is similar in size to the White-sided and occurs in much the same

84

range. Its most distinguishing feature is its white beak. There is also a white area on its back just behind the dorsal fin.

The Pacific Striped Dolphin, seen regularly in West Coast marine exhibits, is common in coastal waters during winter and spring months. It moves offshore to cooler waters in summer and autumn.

Still other members of the same group (all of which have very short snouts, strong flippers, and distinct ridges behind the high dorsal fin and the anus) are: the little-known Wilson's Hourglass Dolphin that lives in Antarctic waters; Fitzroy's Dolphin, found off South America; and the Dusky Dolphin, which is the most common dolphin of New Zealand waters.

RISSO'S DOLPHIN, OR GRAMPUS, occurs in both the Atlantic and the Pacific. The name Grampus is derived from a shortening of two French words (*grand poisson*) that literally mean "big fish."

Pelorus Jack, the best-known Risso's Dolphin and one of the most famous of all dolphins, lived on the ship route between Nelson and Wellington in New Zealand. For two decades, Pelorus Jack met nearly every ship traveling between the islands and escorted them for several miles, riding the bow wave or cavorting alongside. In recognition

of this faithful volunteer's service as a pilot, the New Zealand legislature granted Pelorus Jack full governmental protection.

Risso's Dolphin measures about 12 feet long. It is gray above and nearly white below, and its fins and tail are black. The dorsal fin is high and recurved, and the flippers are long and curved. Risso's Dolphin has no beak, and the forehead rises adruptly from the jaws. There are no teeth in the upper jaw and only a few (three to seven) in each half of the lower jaw.

PILOT WHALE males may measure to 20 feet long or longer, the females shorter. They are also called Blackfish because of their uniformly black color, though they have a white patch under the chin. This broad band of white narrows to a slim white line along the stomach. The high, broad-based dorsal fin is located almost exactly in the middle of the back. The flippers are slim and pointed. The beak is extremely short, and the forehead protrudes into a bulbous or melonlike bulge. Several species occur in warm and temperate seas, and they travel in schools. They were heavily harvested by whale hunters as a source of oil and meat, and they are still hunted in the Faroe Islands.

The name Pilot Whale refers to the animals' habit of following a leader, even when led into shallows where they become beached. There the heavy animals suffocate because their chest cavities are crushed by their body weight, collapsing the lungs. Not uncommonly a whole school of Pilot Whales will follow their leader onto a beach.

The animals may make a bellowing noise when they surface. Whalers imitated the calls to lure the animals into shallow waters, and the imitated sound also became another common name—Caa'ing—that was used by some of the whalers to describe their quarry.

KILLER WHALE, OR ORCA, was long considered the most voracious of all animals in the sea, and indeed it can be. A swift swimmer, it travels in packs of a few to as many as 50 or more animals. They work together, herding and harassing their intended prey until it tires. Then they move in to make a kill. Sharks, seals, penguins, dolphins, whales—no animal in the sea can escape a hungry pack of Killer Whales on the prowl, and their slaughter may at times exceed their own immediate needs.

The Killer Whale roams the oceans throughout the world but is most common in cooler seas. It often appears along coasts. Sometimes a Killer Whale will literally stand on its tail, sticking its head out of the water and looking at its surroundings. When it dives, it may remain submerged for as long as half an hour.

A male Killer Whale may measure 30 feet long. A female is at least a third smaller. The dorsal fin is very large—as high as 6 feet in older males—and it protrudes from the water as the animals swim speedily along near the surface. The flippers are blunt, the flukes very broad, and there is no beak. Basically black, the Killer Whale has a lens-shaped white spot behind each eye and patches of white under the chin, on the belly, and behind the dorsal fin on each side of the streamlined body.

Despite its reputation as a ferocious creature, there are no records of a Killer Whale attacking a human. In recent years this giant beast has been easily tamed, rivaling other dolphins in both docility and responsiveness to training. Now several marine exhibits proudly feature Killer Whales as star attractions and performers (p. 28).

KILLER WHALE

FALSE KILLER WHALE

FALSE KILLER WHALE measures about 15 feet long, the male and female almost the same size. Unlike the Killer Whale, its flippers are slim and pointed rather than blunt. The dorsal fin is small and curved backward, and the color is totally black. It has no beak. Like the Killer Whale, it is common in temperate and tropical seas throughout the world, but it prefers the deep waters of the open ocean where it makes its meals of squid and fish. Like the Pilot Whale (p. 88), with which it is sometimes confused, herds of these animals have been stranded on beaches. Shifting currents may cause them to stray into shallow seas.

ROUGH-TOOTHED DOLPHIN, about 7 feet long, lives in the warm waters of the Atlantic, Pacific, and Indian oceans. Schools of 100 or more have been reported, but little is known about this dolphin's habits. It is bluish black above and pinkish white with slate-colored spots below. Long-beaked Dolphin is another name sometimes used for the Rough-toothed Dolphin. This dolphin and its close relatives are sometimes placed in a separate family, Stenidae. All have a long beak, numerous teeth, and a distinct dorsal fin.

The Brazilian Dolphin, or Tucuxi, lives in fresh water far

ROUGH-TOOTHED DOLPHIN

up the Amazon and other rivers in South and Central America. Bluish black above and pale below, it is only about 4 feet long. Four similar small dolphins inhabit the coastal waters of northeastern South America and may ascend the large rivers.

The Indo-Pacific Humpback Dolphin travels the rivers and coastal waters of the Indian and Pacific oceans off southern Africa, Asia, and Australia. It feeds on fish, despite persistent reports that it is a vegetarian. Several other similar species of dolphins inhabit the rivers and coastal waters of Africa and India.

INDO-PACIFIC HUMPBACK DOLPHIN

RIVER DOLPHINS

Family Platanistidae

These dolphins left the sea, their ancestral home, to live in freshwater lakes and rivers. The bones in their neck are large and separate, as in land mammals. All have a long, slim beak, many teeth, and short, broad flippers.

SUSU, OR INDIA RIVER DOLPHIN, about 8 feet long and almost totally blind, subsists on fish and freshwater shrimp. Its forehead rises sharply from the snout, and its flippers are large and broad based. The fluke is distinctly notched. This dark brown to black dolphin is found only in India in the Ganges and Indus rivers and their tributaries. When it spouts, it makes a noise ("soo-soo") much like its name.

BAIJI, OR CHINESE RIVER DOLPHIN, lives in the lower reaches of the Chang Jiang (Yangtze) River in China. About 7 feet long, it is gray above and white below. The foot-long beak curves up at the tip. Like the Susu, the Baiji is nearly blind. It travels in herds of fewer than half a dozen animals and is an endangered species. Once it was called White Flag Dolphin because it was believed that, when the dolphin swam close to the surface, its large dorsal fin protruding from the water resembled a flag.

97

FRANCISCANA, OR LA PLATA DOLPHIN, rarely more than 5 feet long, lives in coastal waters off eastern South America. The dorsal fin is well developed, and the beak is long and slim. This brownish dolphin feeds on small fish, squid, and crustaceans in the brackish waters. Unlike all other river dolphins, it has good vision.

BOUTU, OR AMAZON DOLPHIN, 6 to 8 feet long, lives in the river basins of eastern South America, 1,000 miles from the sea. Groups generally consist of fewer than half a

FRANCISCANA

dozen animals. Some Boutus are black above and creamy pink or flesh-colored below; others, presumably more mature, are totally cream-colored or pink. The long, slightly down-curved snout bears a few bristles; the dorsal fin is small. The eyes are tiny but still functional. The position of the small eyes above the bulging cheeks prevents the dolphin from looking downward, however, and so when it feeds, it often swims upside down close to the bottom. Both the flippers and the flukes are large. These dolphins have been protected locally by superstition and myths.

BOUTU

99

MANATEES AND DUGONG

Order Sirenia

Totally aquatic, not even coming ashore to breed or to give birth to their young, the manatees and Dugong are found only in warm seas, estuaries, and rivers. These large, timid beasts have a spindle-shaped, bulky body, paddlelike front legs (flippers), and no hind flippers. The flattened tail is the principal means of swimming, though the flippers may be used for steering or for sculling. These are heavy-bodied, dense-boned animals. Though not swift swimmers, they can maneuver skillfully. They have a rounded head, small eyes, and large, flexible, bristly lips. A few stiff hairs are scattered over the thick hide, beneath which is a heavy layer of blubber. The nostrils are on the top of the snout and are kept closed by valves when the animals are underwater.

Strictly plant eaters, consuming as much as 100 pounds of vegetation per day, sirenians have a complex stomach, much like a cow's or other ruminant's. Because their flesh is good to eat, many of these animals were slaughtered by people living along seacoasts. Because they are slow moving, they are often hit and killed by boat propellers, their worst foe today.

Ironically, these ugly animals are said to have helped inspire the mermaid myth, which explains why they are known as sirens. Sailors who equated their looks with feminine beauty, however, had unquestionably been at sea much too long. They are also called sea cows, a more apt name considering their appearance and the use of their flesh as food. Their ancestry shows a clear relationship to elephants and to hyraxes (small land-dwelling mammals of Africa).

solid bone in rib

spongy bone in rib

MANATEES

Family Trichechidae

MANATEES live in tropical and subtropical waters. The West Indian Manatee inhabits the coastal waters and rivers from Florida throughout much of the Caribbean. The Amazon Manatee lives along the coast of Brazil and up such large rivers as the Amazon and the Orinoco. A third species, the West African Manatee, is found in the warm coastal waters off western Africa.

Manatees may measure more than 10 feet long and weigh as much as half a ton, though they are usually smaller. The tail is rounded and has no notch. The front flippers, which still bear rudiments of nails, are so movable that they can be used like arms when the animal wants to pull the front of its body onto a shore to graze briefly on plants. The young swim mainly by using their flippers, but adults use their flippers only for steering and get the power for swimming from their tail.

Manatees have a squared-off muzzle with highly flexible lips that are split in the middle, each half independently movable. The lips are used with dexterity in pulling plants from the bottom or along shore. Even the insides of the lips are bristly, forming brushes that help move food back to the flattened teeth for chewing before it is swallowed.

Manatees are sensitive to cold and will die in prolonged exposure to water that is lower than 70° F. Generally the animals are solitary, but during periods of cold, groups of a dozen or more may assemble in warm springs or in places where there is a flow of warm water from factories or power plants. If the cold comes on so quickly that they have not had time to move, they will die from exposure. A manatee, like a Dugong, surfaces regularly for a new sup-

WEST INDIAN MANATEE

ply of oxygen. If it becomes beached, it will try to roll onto its back to achieve more comfort. Otherwise it will suffocate due to the pressure of its heavy body on its rib cage, as happens also with beached whales.

Manatee cows give birth to one calf that is nursed for about two years before the cow can give birth again. This slow rate of reproduction makes it extremely difficult for manatees to increase their population level, and explains why they are endangered.

103

DUGONG

Family Dugongidae

DUGONG is the only species in its family. It lives in warm coastal waters of the Indian, South Pacific, and North Pacific oceans, this habitat affording it some protection from sharks (though not from people).

About 9 feet long and rarely weighing more than 800 pounds, the Dugong is smaller and more streamlined than

are manatees. Its wedge-shaped tail is deeply notched at the midline. The front flippers show no evidence of nails. Males have two tusks (the upper incisors) that may be as much as 10 inches long. Females bear a single calf every other year.

Normally a Dugong comes to the surface every five or ten minutes to replenish its oxygen supply. Ordinarily it feeds at night. Its world population is only a few thousands. Many are killed by hunters, others by boats or by the destruction of their habitat.

STELLER'S SEA COW

Family Hydromalidae

STELLER'S SEA COW lived in the cold waters of the North Pacific. It grew to a length of more than 20 feet and weighed as much as 6 tons—much larger than any of the living manatees.

Until 1741, this giant was unknown. In that year it was discovered by a Russian expedition and named for Georg Steller, the German naturalist who was serving as chief scientist on the expedition. Forced to spend the winter on the bleak Commander Islands in the Bering Sea between Alaska and northeastern Asia after their ship wrecked, the

106

explorers found the huge, ugly, wrinkly sea cows a tasty food, and they reported this to others who plied the waters.

The original world population of Steller's Sea Cow was probably no more than 2,000 animals, but by 1768, only slightly more than a quarter of a century after its discovery, all had been killed, mainly by whalers, hunters, and explorers following the Russian expedition. Hope that some may have escaped and built a new population is sometimes bolstered by sightings, but these have so far proved to be whales rather than Steller's Sea Cows.

Steller's Sea Cow had an extraordinarily small head for such a large animal. Its skin was rough and almost scaly, and its curiously bent flippers were sparsely covered with hair.

107

SEA LIONS, WALRUSES, AND SEALS

Order Pinnipedia

Fin-footed, or pinniped, mammals, about 30 species, are so closely related to the carnivores (p. 144) that some biologists classify them in the same order.

Pinnipeds have a streamlined body that makes swimming easy. All move clumsily on land. Their feet are flipperlike, with webs between the toes. The tail is very short. Some have small external ears, others none. Both their ears and nostrils can be closed tightly when the animals dive. Pinnipeds are not, however, as completely adapted to an aquatic existence as are the cetaceans and the sirenians, and they must return to land (or to ice) to give birth to their young and to care for them until they are old enough to take to the sea. A thick layer of fat, or blubber, just under the skin insulates them from the cold water.

All pinnipeds are excellent swimmers and can dive deeply, some regularly to 200 feet and one kind—the Elephant Seal—to more than 4,000 feet! The Weddell Seal has been recorded at a depth of 2,000 feet. It can remain submerged for nearly an hour. Before a pinniped dives, it exhales most of the air in its lungs. With most of the air exhausted, it has almost no nitrogen that can be dissolved in its blood, and so it does not develop "bends" (or pressure disease) when it surfaces rapidly. Pinnipeds also have a greater volume of blood per body weight than do land animals, and so they carry a larger amount of oxygen. In dives, however, their heart rate (and therefore the utilization of oxygen) is slowed, and the oxygen is supplied only to essential organs.

Pinnipeds live in all seas throughout the world except in the northern part of the Indian Ocean, but they are most

Seals dive and swim expertly but must surface to breathe air.

abundant in cool waters. The hunting of them goes back beyond written history. Their thick fur made warm clothes and shelters. Their rich meat stoked hungry stomachs and gave fuel for inner warmth in the cold. The bones and teeth were carved into implements and ornaments.

The few people who lived near enough to the coast to harvest these animals for their personal needs took all they needed without threatening the total population. But when great schooners ventured into the waters and began hauling meat and hides to ports throughout the world, slaughtering half a million or more animals every year, the populations of these animals began to dwindle alarmingly. Governments now control the number that can be harvested.

A major threat to pinnipeds today are commercial fishermen, for seals become hopelessly entangled in their nets and drown. The fishermen, of course, complain that the pinnipeds consume "more than a fair share" of the available fish.

Trained and Tamed

Sea lions and seals are trained to put on performances in circuses and marine exhibits. Their repertoires are limited, consisting primarily of balancing balls or other objects on their noses, using their noses to trigger horns to play tunes, and applauding themselves with a vigorous clapping of their flippers. For this they get a reward of fish. These are essentially aquatic animals, of course, but they do their tricks on land. "At home" in the water they would be more comfortable and could be more spectacular.

After balancing a ball on its nose, a seal will clap its flippers as if applauding.

EARED SEALS

Family Otariidae

Members of this family are more like land carnivores than are the other pinnipeds. They still have small external ears, for example, which are totally lacking in the more stream-lined members of the family Phocidae (p. 128). Eared seals also have longer necks and are thus not as compact in body form as their more aquatic cousins. They can move on land more easily than other pinnipeds, however, for they can turn their hind flippers forward to support their body. Their flippers are naked.

All eared seals are gregarious, particularly during the breeding season. Bulls, which are much larger than the cows, maintain many females in "harems" and do not feed during the months when their harems and territories must be guarded.

NORTHERN FUR SEAL lives in large colonies in the North Pacific and adjacent seas, mainly on the Pribilof Islands off Alaska. It migrates in the fall and winter as far southward as waters off Japan and southern California. Of all the seals, none has fur more prized. The long, dark brown guard hairs are removed to expose the fine, thick chestnut underfur, the popular "sealskin" of commerce.

In spring these seals migrate northward to their breeding islands. The bulls, which may be 6 to 7 feet long and weigh as much as 700 pounds, arrive first, in late April or in May. They go ashore to establish claim to their positions on the islands. Each selects a territory somewhere near the shore. Most bulls return to the same spot year after year. A bull must be powerful enough to defend his claim against other bulls that may decide they want the same location.

A large colony of Northern Fur Seals on an island off the coast of Alaska.

Cows, only one-fourth the weight of the bulls, reach the islands a month or so later. Mature females are already pregnant from mating the year before. Bulls greet them at the shore and coerce them into joining the harem. A large, strong bull may succeed in building a harem of 50 or more females. Weaker bulls capture fewer females for their harems and do not get the choice spots on the island.

Bachelor males too young to mate and not yet strong enough to compete with the big bulls stay apart from the breeding colony in small groups of their own.

Within a few hours to a few days after their arrival, each pregnant female gives birth to a single pup. All the while their burly, boisterous mates stand guard to prevent any cows from straying out of the harem and to block roaming males that may try to enter. Fights with other males are frequent. The big bulls trust no one and will not leave even long enough to get meals. They survive by living on their stored fat. Their constant brawling vigil is continued for as long as two months, during which time the bulls also mate with the females. Finally, the mating over for the year and the families almost ready to put out to sea again, the big bulls relax and leave their posts. By this time, the bulls are thin and weak, with only enough strength remaining to get back into the water.

The stage is now set for the young females that have

NORTHERN FUR SEAL

never mated before to be selected by bachelor bulls and by bulls that lost their earlier claims to territories. These virgin females, now two to four years old, move in from the sea and pair off with bulls.

The black-furred pups stay with their mothers around the clock for about a week. Then the mothers mate and go out to sea for about a week to feed. The pups play together and can swim before they are two months old. They do most of their growing up without attention from their mothers. When a pup's mother does come ashore, she calls for her offspring. When her pup appears—many that are not

bull

cow

115

pup

hers will try to nurse—she identifies her own by its call and its odor and allows only it to nurse. Within about three months, the pups are weaned.

Winter is now coming on, and the whole colony straggles out to sea. Some will travel thousands of miles southward to reach their wintering waters. They move singly or in small groups rather than in a large group. Killer Whales and sharks prey on them along the way. More than half of the pups will die from exposure, disease, or predation before reaching their second birthday.

116

cows with pups

Humans have been the most ravaging of the predators. The massacre of seals to obtain their skins made millionaires of commercial furriers but nearly exterminated the seals, reducing the herds from a total population of possibly 3 million to fewer than 300,000. Now, by international agreement, the seals are protected on their breeding grounds and at sea. Their population is slowly increasing again, totaling more than a million. Harvests are mainly of young males, for these have the best fur. Cows and bulls are saved for breeding, which sustains the species.

GUADALUPE FUR SEAL was once abundant in Pacific coastal waters from San Francisco, California, southward to Guadalupe Island, Mexico. Early in the 1800s, it was nearly exterminated by fur hunters. Near the end of the century, it was rediscovered on Guadalupe Island. For the second time hunters nearly killed it off, and no more were seen until around 1925. Somewhere in the sea and on the rocky shores, however, a few had escaped and thus saved the species. Now protected, a small colony consisting of a few hundred of these handsome seals is once again slowly building in numbers on Guadalupe Island.

The Guadalupe Fur Seal resembles the Northern Fur Seal but has a more sharply pointed nose. Bulls may weigh as much as 500 pounds and measure 6 feet long.

OTHER FUR SEALS include seven species closely related to the Guadalupe Fur Seal. All of them live in the Southern Hemisphere.

They breed in the cool waters along the southern coasts of South America, Africa, Australia, and New Zealand and on small oceanic islands. One species regularly visits shores only a few hundred miles from icy Antarctica.

CALIFORNIA SEA LION, to 8 feet long and weighing more than 600 pounds, breeds along the rocky Pacific shores from southern California to northern Mexico, but wanders as far north as British Columbia. A colony is also found on the Galapagos Islands, off the coast of Ecuador. Large males command harems in breeding colonies.

The California Sea Lion's face bears no resemblance to a lion's. To most people, it looks more doglike or bearlike. Males have a bristly mane, however, which is the probable reason for the lion part of the animal's name. Males also have a crest of hair on their high forehead. In the wild, the California Sea Lion eats fish, squid, and other sea creatures that it catches underwater.

When its body is dry, which is rare, the California Sea Lion is a rich brown. When wet, it appears black. This is the common "trained seal" exhibited in zoos, circuses, and oceanariums.

COW

bull

NORTHERN, OR STELLER'S, SEA LION is about twice the size of the California Sea Lion, measuring as much as 10 feet long. Very large bulls can weigh up to a ton, females about three-quarters of a ton. This species breeds from southern California to the Bering Sea and Soviet islands.

Bulls have manes like the California Sea Lion, but they lack the head crest. They are light, almost yellowish brown.

Unlike the California Sea Lion, this species does not respond easily to taming, and so it is rare in captivity. The Northern Sea Lion is wary in the wild, plunging into the water quickly if it is on shore and then diving out of sight.

OTHER SEA LIONS include the South American Sea Lion found on the Falkland Islands and in the Straits of Magellan northward along both coasts of South America to Peru

cow

pup

and Uruguay. Males measure about 8 feet long and weigh approximately 1,000 pounds; females are a third smaller. This seal is mainly an animal of the sea, but it occasionally swims up rivers. It inhabits such rocky, stormy shores that it has not been overhunted. It lives in groups that become organized harems during the breeding season. Adult males are dark brown, the females gray. In both sexes, the belly is cream to yellow. Males have a distinct mane.

Australian Sea Lion lives along the southern coast of Australia and on islands south of New Zealand.

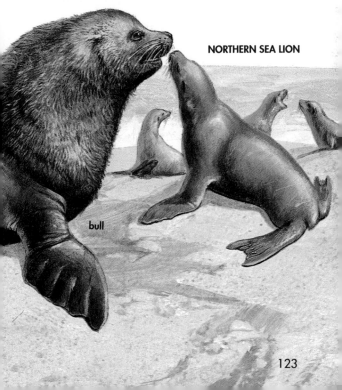

NORTHERN SEA LION

bull

WALRUSES

Family Odobenidae

WALRUSES, one of the most familiar of all sea animals and the only member of its family, lives in a bleak land where there are few people—the shallow, cold arctic seas. Walruses spend their summers in the Chukchi Sea, then travel southward in autumn to winter in the Bering Sea.

In times past the Walrus was as important to the Eskimos as the bison were to the Plains Indians. It provided them with food. Its blubber was used for waterproofing, its oil for lights. The thick hide covered boats and dwellings,

124

and the ivory tusks were carved to make tools, weapons, and ornaments.

In addition to people, the Walrus contends with only two other enemies, the Polar Bear and the Killer Whale. The Polar Bear is not a match for a full-grown Walrus. But if a mother Walrus can be harassed into letting her young get away from her protective bulk, a Polar Bear makes a meal of the pudgy youngster. At sea, the Walrus must beware of hungry packs of Killer Whales. It is rare, in fact, for a Walrus to go far out to sea. Much of its time is spent on the ice, and it hunts for food on the bottom of shallow seas.

A full-grown male Walrus may be 12 feet long and

weigh as much as 3,000 pounds, a third more than the female. Its tusks may be 3 feet long, occasionally longer, and they may each weigh 15 pounds or more. Both males and females have tusks, but those of the female are shorter and not as heavy. Walruses use their tusks as levers to lift themselves onto the ice. These become prods to get neighbors to move out of the way, or they can be formidable weapons in battling attackers or in spars with competitors of their own species. Using their tusks, Walruses dig in the bottom of the water for clams, their principal food. The shells are crushed with the giant, grinding teeth and then the soft parts sucked out. The indigestible shell is spit out. A Walrus may feast on 500 or more clams at a meal.

A large, mature Walrus has almost no hair on its thick, wrinkly skin. What hair it has is heavy and reddish. The sensitive whiskers around its mouth are almost as stiff as coat-hanger wires. The head is round, the eyes small, and the ear openings covered with small flaps of skin. The hind flippers can be turned forward so that the animal can walk on land, as in eared seals (p. 111). Both the front and the hind flippers are hairless on the underside but are covered with hair above. The digits on the flippers bear small claws.

A female Walrus gives birth to a single calf every two years. The calf stays with its mother for about two years and continues to nurse until it sets out on its own.

In a colony, which may contain hundreds of individuals, the animals are generally quite peaceful. The larger animals spend most of their time sleeping. A Walrus can inflate the pouches on each side of its throat to make "floats" that help hold its head above water while it is sleeping at sea. If a Walrus is awakened by a passerby, it bellows loudly and brandishes its tusks—but soon goes back to its snoozing.

WALRUS

These ornaments were carved from Walrus tusks, c. 1865-1893.

127

EARLESS SEALS

Family Phocidae

Of the pinnipeds, these seals are best adapted for a fully aquatic existence. As their name indicates, their streamlining has evolved to the stage where they lack external ears. This feature and their compact, seemingly neckless body help to reduce resistance when the animals are moving through the water. In swimming, they are the most fishlike of the seals. Because the hind flippers are directed to the rear and cannot be pivoted forward for support, the animals travel awkwardly on land or ice. They move by "humping" their body and dragging their hind quarters forward.

Like all pinnipeds, these seals must leave the water to breed and to rear their young. The young can take to the water within a few weeks after birth. Some of these pinnipeds can stay underwater for more than an hour in their deep dives in search of fish and squid, at least one going down to more than 4,000 feet. Although earless seals have underhairs, these are never so abundant as to compose a "fur." Nevertheless, hunters have taken a heavy toll of many species in their search for meat, oil, hides, and the pelts of newborn pups.

MONK SEALS, from 6 to 9 feet long, are the only tropical pinnipeds.

The Mediterranean Monk Seal, found in the Mediterranean and along the northwestern coast of Africa, is rare. Probably no more than 1,000 animals still exist. The Caribbean Monk Seal, once fairly common, was hunted to extinction sometime in the early 1900s. Most of these seals were killed for food. The Hawaiian Monk Seal, dark brown

HAWAIIAN MONK SEAL

above and paler below, is also in serious danger of extinction. Its total population in the 1980s was fewer than 1,500, about half its level in 1960 when, as a result of protection, its numbers were believed to be increasing. None of the monk seals has been able to tolerate intrusion by humans.

HARBOR SEAL, the common seal of temperate to cold seas in the Northern Hemisphere, is easily recognized by its spotted coat. Normally the spots are black on a yellowish-gray background, but some animals are black with white spots. An adult male Harbor Seal measures about 5 feet long and weighs about 150 to 250 pounds. The females are nearly as large as the males. The single pup, born in spring or early summer, wears a spotted gray coat similar to, though paler than, the coat of its mother.

Harbor Seals assemble in groups of up to several hundred. They do not congregate in breeding colonies of many

130

thousands as do the fur seals. This has helped to spare the animals from slaughter, for their limited commercial value makes it uneconomical to hunt them individually.

Harbor Seals commonly come ashore to sleep, but they may also sleep on the bottom in shallow water, rising every quarter of an hour or so to get a fresh supply of air—all without waking up. Their food is fish, squid, crustaceans, and mollusks. They may dive to depths of 250 feet or more and remain submerged for a quarter of an hour or longer. Generally, however, they stay close to shore. They are extremely wary.

131

HARP SEAL bulls may be more than 6 feet long and weigh as much as 400 pounds. Although as many as 100,000 of these seals are killed every year, they number in the millions in the North Atlantic. Newborn pups, called "whitecoats" by sealers, are covered with a snow-white fur that is lost in less than a month and replaced with ash-gray fur. In adults, a band of black extends from the black head back along each side, roughly outlining a saddle shape that is most prominent in mature males. These seals feed mainly on fish but will also make a meal of crabs or other crustaceans if they are available.

RINGED SEAL, about 5 feet long, is the smallest of all seals. It lives in the Arctic Ocean and adjacent seas. When the ocean freezes, this seal keeps a small hole open where it surfaces to breathe. The Ringed Seal is gray with dark patches outlined with a lighter color. In some individuals, the dark patches run together on the back. This is an abundant seal, as the population is possibly greater than 3 million.

The closely related Baikal Seal lives the year-round in freshwater Lake Baikal in Siberia. Another, the Caspian Seal, inhabits the brackish inland Caspian Sea.

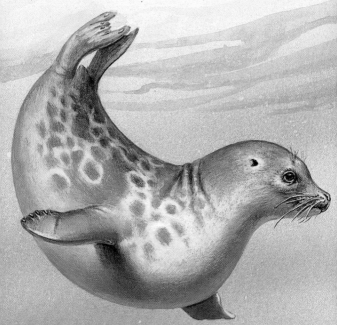

RIBBON SEAL lives in icy waters between Alaska and Siberia. The total population is now believed to be about 50,000. Large bulls may be 6 feet long and weigh 150 to 200 pounds. The females are smaller and not as brightly colored. Eskimos have always prized the unusual and naturally decorated hides of these seals. The basic color is dark brown or black, with light bands circling the neck, each flipper, and the rear of the body. Banded Seal is another name for this rare seal.

cow

pup

bull

GRAY SEAL is found in temperate waters of the North Atlantic, preferring rocky shores. Bulls, which may be 10 feet long and weigh as much as 650 pounds, command a selected rocky site to which they lure females into a loose "harem" during the breeding season. They allow the females to wander to the sites of other bulls, however.

The bulls usually have three deep neck wrinkles. Both sexes are dark brown with light-colored bellies. They both look jet black when wet. Like the Harp Seals, the pups are gray when first born, but this birthday suit is replaced by a blue-gray coat within three or four weeks. Females are ready to bear young when they are two years old, but males do not mature for six or seven years. Fortunately for the species, these seals do not have great commercial value.

135

CRABEATER SEAL, about 8 feet long, lives on fast-ice in the Antarctic. In summer its coat is gray; in winter it is white. This seal can "wiggle" across smooth snow and ice almost as fast as a person can run.

The Crabeater Seal forms a sieve of its lobed teeth to catch krill, the small shrimplike crustaceans so plentiful in Antarctic waters. The krill are its principal food. Despite its name, it does not eat crabs.

The total number of these seals is estimated to be 5 to 15 million, making it the most abundant of all seals. The seals generally live at the edge of the pack ice and so are in this sense semi-migratory.

LEOPARD SEAL, up to 10 feet long and weighing as much as 1,000 pounds, spends its time in the cold waters of the Antarctic. In winter, stragglers may move northward to warmer waters.

As its name suggests, this seal's coat is spotted, black on gray. Some are wholly black above but are lighter below. The Leopard Seal's head seems long compared to its rather slim body. It eats penguins (the mainstay food), fish, and squid. The Leopard Seal is more solitary than the other seals of the Antarctic region. It is nowhere abundant and is reported from scattered locations northward to the tips of Africa, South America, and Australia.

ROSS SEAL

ROSS SEAL is rarely sighted. It lives on pack ice fringing the Antarctic but does not winter under the ice. It feeds mainly on squid. The coarse fur is greenish yellow above and lighter below. Because of this seal's large eyes, it also goes by the name of Big-eyed Seal. This seal's well-developed flippers are evidence that it is a skilled, swift swimmer. The Ross Seal may reach a length of 8 feet and weigh as much as 500 pounds.

bull

cow

143

CARNIVORES

Order Carnivora

This large order includes dogs, cats, raccoons, otters, skunks, weasels, foxes, and other less familiar animals. Some of them, such as raccoons and otters, may hunt along shores and occasionally venture into the water, but only two species—the Sea Otter and the Polar Bear—depend for a living on seafood.

OTTERS, WEASELS, AND THEIR KIN

Family Mustelidae

SEA OTTER, to 5 feet long including the tail and weighing as much as 100 pounds, spends its entire life at sea. The Sea Otter is the largest member of the weasel family. Its thick, glossy, dark-brown fur—white-tipped in old animals—was considered so valuable that the Sea Otter was hunted to near extinction. As the otters became scarce, the price of their pelts even before 1900 rose to more than $2,000 each. During the early 1900s, it was not believed

that the species would survive, but small, hidden breeding groups persisted on the California coast and in Alaska's Aleutian Islands. Under protection, the Sea Otter is making a comeback. The world population was about 150,000 in 1989.

The Sea Otter seldom comes to shore. It rests and sleeps on its back at sea, commonly in the floating kelp to which it clings. The Sea Otter spends much of its time hunting food and eating, which is necessary to provide the energy it needs for its nearly constant swimming. It may eat as much as 20 percent of its body weight every day. It feeds on shellfish and fish, sometimes diving to a depth of 300 feet to get them. It can crush sea urchins and clams in its pow-

SEA OTTER

erful teeth. Often, however, it brings a rock to the surface and rests it on its stomach for use as an "anvil" on which to crack the shells. This is a rare example of a nonhuman animal using a tool.

Females, smaller than the males, give birth at sea every year or so to a single pup. A young otter—weighing 4 to 5 pounds and the smallest at birth of all marine mammals—is fully furred and capable of swimming at birth. The mother gives it great care, nursing it for nearly a year. When nursing, the mother floats on her back and holds the young in her paws. She also allows it to sleep on her belly as she floats.

out with her young, usually weaning them in April. The cubs stay with their mother for more than a year before they set out on their own. By this time they may weigh 200 pounds or more.

Polar Bears are not streamlined in body form as are the cetaceans, sirenians, and pinnipeds, but they nevertheless do well in the water. They are skilled and tireless swimmers and have been seen more than 100 miles out at sea.

WHALE WATCHING

More than a million people go whale watching every year. One expedition originated in 1975 when a sixth-grade class at Provincetown Elementary School in Massachusetts accepted an invitation for a free boat trip to see whales off Cape Cod. Only one small whale and a dolphin were seen that year, but it was a beginning. That same boat operator now takes out approximately 100,000 people every year. Along the northeastern coast of the United States and Canada, more than three dozen other whale-watching boats are in operation. Some trips last only a few hours, others a week or longer. At least a dozen boats also take people seal watching. Scientists from research centers commonly go on these excursions to photograph and to study sea mammals.

Similar trips can be taken along the west coast of the United States and Canada. People crowd the rails when whales are sighted, exclaiming excitedly and appreciatively. Pictures are taken, an excursion leader lectures, and the boats are maneuvered to give passengers the best possible views while not disturbing the animals.

All of this has added much to people's understanding of and affection for whales and their kin, but some authorities question whether watching harms the animals. Their natural behavior is somewhat disrupted, and there is genuine concern that this can be a serious threat to their well-being. Sometimes, too, the animals are unintentionally hit by boat propellers and seriously harmed. Trying to satisfy their customers, some skippers used to cruise quietly up to a sleeping whale, then make a loud noise by beating on the side of the boat or gunning the motor. Frightened awake, the whale often did things that delighted the watchers—diving suddenly, leaping out of the water, or spouting. This is but one example of intrusion. Seals were similarly disturbed by well-intentioned but nevertheless extremely obtrusive observers. Such harassment has been illegal since the signing of the Marine Mammal Protection Act in 1972.

Watching from shore or from an anchored vessel can be rewarding and can be done unobtrusively, for the animals are not even aware they are being observed. The big Gray Whales migrating along the California coast, for example, come close enough to shore to be seen easily, particularly with a telescope or a pair of binoculars. For most people this kind of observation is satisfying enough. They do not need to touch the animals to enjoy them. They are happy to see the whales and other marine mammals doing what they normally do in their own world—and this is as it should be.

Many people enjoy whale watching, although it can threaten the animals' privacy.

ANIMAL WELFARE ORGANIZATIONS

Until the 1970s the welfare of marine mammals concerned only a few people. Now the concerned number in the millions. People almost everywhere in the world have an affection for these mammals. For some species, this attention may have come too late to save them from extinction, but for others it is indeed salvation.

All maritime nations have special agencies that deal with marine mammals. In the United States these include the federal government and the governments of coastal states. The National Marine Fisheries Service of the Department of Commerce is responsible for whales, dolphins, porpoises, seals, and sea lions; the Fish and Wildlife Service of the Department of the Interior looks after the Walrus, Sea Otter, Polar Bear, Manatee, and Dugong (the last only at Palau). The Marine Mammal Commission, established by Congress in 1972, reviews the status of all marine mammal populations, encourages research, and makes recommendations regarding federal activities that affect marine mammals. The International Whaling Commission (p. 24) establishes policies for whaling in international waters, but enforcement is left to each nation's conscience.

Private organizations have been the most valuable in alerting the public to the plight of marine mammals. Through films distributed to schools and civic organizations and shown on television, they have created worldwide sympathy for marine mammals. Some of these organizations also monitor proposed legislation and the enforcement of existing laws. Through several of these private groups you can "adopt" an individual whale or manatee, receiving as you do so its life history, adoption papers, and a picture. Your adoption money is used for research and education. These groups—whatever they do and however they go about it—offer "life insurance" to marine mammal species.

Among the many organizations that feature marine mammal protection are the following:

American Cetacean Society
P.O. Box 2639
San Pedro, CA 90731

Animal Welfare Institute
P.O. Box 3650
Washington, DC 20007

Center for Environmental
Education, Inc.
624 9th Street, NW
Washington, DC 20001

Dolphin Research Center
P. O. Box 2875
Marathon Shores, FL 33052

Friends of the Sea Otter
P.O. Box 221220
Carmel, CA 93922

Greenpeace, Inc.
1436 U Street, NW
Washington, DC 20009

Pacific Whale Foundation
P.O. Box 1083
Kihei, Maui, HI 96753

Save the Manatee Club
500 N. Maitland Avenue
Suite 210
Maitland, FL 32751

Sea Shepherd Conservation
Society
P.O. Box 7000-S
Redondo Beach, CA 90277

Whale Adoption Project
International Wildlife Coalition
634 North Falmouth Highway
Box 388
North Falmouth, MA 02556

Whale Museum
P.O. Box 945
Friday Harbor, WA 98250

Representatives of Greenpeace in small boat confront a Russian factory ship.

MARINE MAMMAL EXHIBITS

Marine mammals are exhibited at major zoos throughout the world, and for half a century they have been featured performers at saltwater aquariums. In the United States these exhibits must be licensed, and they are monitored by both government and private agencies to make certain the animals are given proper care. Most of the exhibits have staff veterinarians and biologists who tend to the needs of the captive animals. These experts also conduct research, and when marine mammals in the wild become stranded or are injured, the experts organize rescue teams and provide housing for the animals.

Major marine mammal exhibits in the United States are listed below. There are also attractions of this sort in Japan, Australia, France, Germany, Great Britain, and other countries. An outstanding attraction in Canada, for example, is the Vancouver Public Aquarium in British Columbia.

Marineland of Florida
9507 Ocean Shore Boulevard
Marineland, FL 32086

Marine World, Africa USA
1000 Fairgrounds Drive
Vallejo, CA 94589

Miami Seaquarium
4400 Rickenbacker Causeway
Miami, FL 33149

Mystic Marine Life Aquarium
55 Coogan Boulevard
Mystic, CT 06355

Ocean World
1701 Southeast 17th Street
Causeway
Fort Lauderdale, FL 33316

Sea Life Park
Makpuu Point
Waumanalo, HI 96795

Seattle Aquarium
Pier 59
Waterfront Park
Seattle, WA 98101

Sea World of California
1720 South Shores Road
San Diego, CA 92109

Sea World of Florida
7007 Sea World Drive
Orlando, FL 32821

Theater of the Sea
P.O. Box 407
Islamorada, FL 33036

MORE INFORMATION

Newspapers and magazines regularly publish articles about marine mammals, and numerous books are available. Many books deal with specific animals, such as the Blue or Sperm whales, or treat particular aspects of the subject, such as whaling or communication. The books listed here are general.

Baker, Mary L. Whales, Dolphins, and Porpoises of the World. Doubleday, New York, 1987.

Caldwell, David K., et al. The Audubon Society Field Guide to North American Fishes, Whales, and Dolphins. Alfred A. Knopf, Inc., New York, 1983.

Cousteau, Jacques-Ives, and Philippe Diole. Dolphins. A and W Visual Library, New York, 1975.

Ellis, Richard. The Book of Whales. Alfred A. Knopf, Inc., New York, 1985.

Ellis, Richard. Dolphins and Porpoises. Alfred A. Knopf, Inc., New York, 1982.

Hoyt, Erich. The Whale-Watcher's Handbook. Doubleday, New York, 1984.

Katona, Steven K., Valerie Rough, and David T. Richardson. Whales, Porpoises, and Seals. Charles Scribner's Sons, New York, 1983.

Leatherwood, Stephen, and Randall R. Reeves. Whales and Dolphins. Sierra Club Books, San Francisco, 1983.

Minasian, Stanley, et al. The World's Whales. Smithsonian Books, Washington, DC, 1984.

Norris, Kenneth S. Whales, Dolphins, and Porpoises. University of California Press, Berkeley, California, 1978.

Scheffer, Victor. Natural History of Marine Mammals. Macmillan, New York, 1981.

Scheffer, Victor. The Year of the Whale. Charles Scribner's Sons, New York, 1969.

SCIENTIFIC NAMES

The following are the scientific names of the marine mammals illustrated in this book. **Heavy** type indicates pages where they appear. The genus name is first, then the species. If the genus name is abbreviated, it is the same as the genus name given just before it.

36-37 Bowhead: Balaena mysticetus
38-39 Right Whale: Eubalaena glacialis
Pygmy: Caperea marginata
40-41 Fin: Balaenoptera physalus
42-43 Blue: B. musculus
46-47 Sei: B. borealis
48-49 Minke: B. acurostris
Bryde's: B. edeni
50-51 Humpback: Megaptera novaeangliae
52-53 Gray: Eschrichtius robustus
55 Goosebeak: Ziphius cavirostris
56-57 Bottlenosed: Hyperoodon ampullatus
58 Baird's: Berardius bairdii
59 Dense-beaked: Mesoplodon densirostris
60-61 Sowerby's Beaked: M. bidens
Straptoothed: M. layardii
62-63 Sperm: Physeter catodon
65 Pygmy: Kogia breviceps
66-67 Narwhal: Monodon monoceros
68-69 White: Delphinapterus leucas
70-71 Harbor: Phocoena phocoena
72-73 Dall's: Phocoenoides dalli
74-75 Finless: Neophocaena phocaenoides
77 Saddleback: Delphinus delphis
78-79 Bottlenosed: Tursiops truncatus
80 Spotted: Stenella plagiodon
81 Commerson's: Cephalorhynchus commersonii
Northern Right-Whale: Lissodelphis borealis
82 Pygmy Killer: Feresa attenuata
83 Irrawaddy: Orcaella brevirostris
84-85 White-sided: Lagenorhynchus acutus

86-87 Risso's: Grampus griseus
88-89 Pilot: Globicephala melaena
90-92 Killer: Orcinus orca
93 False: Pseudorca crassidens
94-95 Rough-toothed: Steno bredanensis
Indo-Pacific: Sousa chinensis
96 Susu: Platanista gangetica
97 Baiji: Lipotes vexillifer
98 Franciscana: Pontoporia blainvillei
99 Bouto: Inia geoffrensis
101, 103 West Indian: Trichechus manatus
104-105 Dugong: Dugong dugon
106-107 Steller's: Hydrodamalis gigas
114-117 Northern: Callorhinus ursinus
118-119 Guadalupe: Arctocephalus townsendii
120-121 California: Zalophus californianus
122-123 Northern: Eumetopias jubatus
124-127 Walrus: Odobenus rosmarus
129 Hawaiian: Monachus schauinslandi
130-131 Harbor: Phoca vitulina
132 Harp: P. groenlandica
133 Ringed: P. hispida
134 Ribbon: P. fasciata
135 Gray: Halichoerus grypus
136 Crabeater: Lobodon carcinophagus
137 Leopard: Hydrurga leptonyx
138-139 Ross: Ommatophoca rossii
Weddell: Leptonychotes weddelli
140 Bearded: Erignathus barbatus
141 Hooded: Crystophora cristata
142-143 Northern Elephant: Mirounga angustirostris
144-147 Sea Otter: Enhydra lutris
149-151 Polar Bear: Ursus maritimus

INDEX

Page numbers in **boldface** indicate pages where a species is identified by description and, in most cases, also illustrated on the same or a facing page. Inclusive page numbers are given for orders, suborders, and families.

Amazon Dolphin, **98**
Amazon Manatee, 102
ambergris, 64
Australian Sea Lion, 123

Baiji, **97**
Baikal Seal, 133
Baird's Whale, **58**
Balaenidae, 36-39
Balaenopteridae, 40-51
baleen, 9, 34, 36, 46, 48, 49, 51
Baleen Whales, 9, 13, 34-53
Banded Seal, 134
Basilosaurus, 8
Beaked Whales, 54-61
Bearded Seal, **140**
Bears, 148-151
Beluga, **68**
Big-eyed Seal, 138
birth, 12
Blackfish, 88
blowholes, 10, 11, 34, 54
blubber, 7, 17, 18, 124
Blue Whale, 6, 11, 13, 17, **42-45**
"bonnet," 38
Bottlenosed Dolphin, **78-79**
Bottlenosed Whale, **56-57**
Boutu, **98-99**
Bowhead Whale, 10, 15, 36, **37**
Brazilian Dolphin, 94-95
breaching, 51
Bryde's Whale, 11, **49**

Caa'ing, 89
California Sea Lion, **120**
Caribbean Monk Seal, 128
Carnivora, 144
Carnivores, 4, 144-151
Caspian Seal, 133
Cetacea, 6-99
cetaceans, 4, 6-99
Chinese River Dolphin, **97**
commercial fishermen, 25, 29, 109
Commerson's Dolphin, **81**
communication, 14
conservation, 24-25
Cowfish, 60
Crab-eater Seal, **136**

Dall's Porpoise, **72-73**

Delphinidae, 76-95
Dense-beaked Whale, **59**
Devilfish, 53
Dolphin Research Center, 25
Dolphins, 26-33, 76-99
Dugongidae, 104-105
Dugong, 100, **104-105**
Dusky Dolphin, 85
Dwarf Sperm Whale, **65**

Eared Seals, 111-123
Earless Seals, 128-143
echolocation, 15
Elephant Seal, 108, 142
Eschrichtidae, 52-53
eyes, 14

factory ships, 21-23
False Killer Whale, **93**
Fin Whale, **40-41**
Fin Whales, 40-51
Fin-footed Mammals, 108-143
Finless Porpoise, **74-75**
Finned Seal, 138
Fitzroy's Dolphin, 85
"Flipper," 27, 79
flukes, 7, 16
fossil, 8
Franciscana, **98**
Fur Seals, 111-119

gams, 17
Goosebeak Whale, **55**
Grampus, **86-87**
Gray Seal, **135**
Gray Whale, 10, 17, **52-53**, 153
Guadalupe Fur Seal, **118**

Harbor Porpoise, **70-71**
Harbor Seal, **130-131**
harpoon, 20, 21
Harp Seal, **132**
Hawaiian Monk Seal, **128**
hearing, 14
hemoglobin, 11
herds, 17, 37
"herring hogs," 29
Hooded Seal, **141**
Humpback Whale, 11, 20, **50-51**
Hydromalidae, 106-107

India River Dolphin, **96**

Indo-Pacific Humpback Dolphin, **95**
International Whaling Commission, 24, 53, 154
Irrawaddy Dolphin, **83**

Killer Whale, 28-29, 30, 54, **90-92**, 125
killing of whales, 18-23
krill, 17, 44, 136

La Plata Dolphin, **98**
Le Jacobite, 81
Leopard Seal, **137**
lobtailing, 51, 84
logging, 16
Long-beaked Dolphin, 94

Mammals, 4-5
Manatees, 100-103
marine exhibits, 27, 30-33, 156
Marineland of Florida, 27
Marine Mammal Commission, 154
Marine Mammal Protection Act, 154
Mediterranean Monk Seal, 128
"melon," 14, 54, 56, 68, 88
Melville, Herman, 63
migration, 17, 53, 153
military use, 33
milk, 4, 13
Minke Whale, **48**
Moby Dick, 63
Monk Seals, **128-129**
Monodontidae, 66-69
Mustelidae, 144-147
Mysticeti, 9, 34-53

Narwhal, **66-67**
National Marine Fisheries Service, 154
Northern Elephant Seal, **142**
Northern Fur Seal, **111-117**
Northern Right-Whale Dolphin, **81**
Northern Sea Lion, **122**
nostrils, 10
nursing, 13

159

Odobenidae, 124-127
Odontoceti, 9, 54-99
oil, 18, 88
Orca, **90-92**
organizations, 154-155
Otariidae, 111-123
Otters, 144-147

Pacific Beaked Whale, 61
Pacific Striped Dolphin, 85
Pelorus Jack, 86-87
performing dolphins, 30-33
Phocidae, 128-143
Phocoenidae, 70
Physeteridae, 62
Piebald Porpoise, 81
Pilot Whale, **88-89**
Pinnipedia, 108-143
pinnipeds, 4, 108-143
Platanistidae, 96-99
pods, 17
Polar Bear, 125, **148-151**
Porpoises, 26, 70-75
Pygmy Killer Whale, **82**
Pygmy Right Whale, **38**
Pygmy Sperm Whale, **65**

Razorback, 40-41
Ribbon Seal, **134**
Right Whale, **38**
Right Whales, 36-39
Ringed Seal, **133**
River Dolphins, 96-99
Risso's Dolphin, **86**
Rorquals, 40-51
Ross Seal, **138**
Rough-toothed Dolphin, **94**

Saddleback Dolphin, **76-77**

scientific names, 158
Sea Canary, 69
sea cow, 2, 100, 106-107
"sea hog," 70
Sea Lions, 108-110, 120-123
Sea Otter, **144-147**
Seals, 108-119, 128-143, 148
seal watching, 152-153
Sea World, 29
Sei Whale, 11, **46-47**
senses, 14
singing, 15, 51
Sirenia, 100-107
sirenians, 4, 100-107
sirens, 15
Skunk Dolphin, 81
sleep, 16
Slender Dolphin, 80
songs, 15
sounds, 14, 43
South American Sea Lion, 122-123
Southern Right-Whale Dolphin, 81
Southern Elephant Seal, 142
Sowerby's Beaked Whale, **60-61**
speed, 16, 47
Sperm Whale, 10, 20, 54, **62-64**
spermaceti, 56, 62, 64
Spinner Dolphin, 80
Spotted Dolphin, **80**
spout, 10, 11, 34
Steller, Georg, 106
Steller's Sea Cow, 2, **106-107**

Steller's Sea Lion, **122**
Stenidae, 94
stranding, 65, 89, 93
Straptoothed Whale, **61**
suckling, 4, 13
Sulphur-bottomed Whale, 44
Susu, **96**
swimming, 16

Toothed Whales, 9, 13, 54-99
trained, 26-33, 110
Trichechidae, 102-103
True's Beaked Whale, 61
True's Porpoise, 73
Tucuxi, 94-95
tuna fishermen, 29
tusks, 66, 126

unicorn, 67
Ursidae, 148-151
U. S. Navy, 33

Walrus, 108, **124-127**, 148
Weddell Seal, **139**
West African Manatee, 102
West Indian Manatee, 102
whalebone, 9, 34
whale watching, 152-153
whaling, 18-23, 40, 41
White-beaked Dolphin, 84-85
White Flag Dolphin, 97
White-sided Dolphin, **84**
White Whale, **68-69**
Wilson's Hourglass Dolphin, 85

Ziphiidae, 54-61.

PHOTO CREDITS: We are indebted to the following photographers and institutions for the photographs used in this book. New Bedford Whaling Museum: 18-19; ACS—G. Bakker/Marine Mammal Images: 22, 23; Laurel Canty/Dolphin Research Center: 25, 32, 153; Marineland of Florida: 26, 27; Miami Seaquarium: 28, 31, 110; Mystic Seaport Museum: 127 (photo inset); Joe Scordino, National Marine Fisheries Service/NOAA: 112-113; Greenpeace/Rex Weyler: 155. We are also indebted to the following institution and photographers for the use of photographs as the basis for illustrations. ACS—G. Bakker/Marine Mammal Images: 20, 21; Mark Conlin/Marine Mammal Images: 109.